Henry Johnston

Chronicles of Glenbuckle

Henry Johnston

Chronicles of Glenbuckle

ISBN/EAN: 9783743349445

Manufactured in Europe, USA, Canada, Australia, Japa

Cover: Foto ©ninafisch / pixelio.de

Manufactured and distributed by brebook publishing software (www.brebook.com)

Henry Johnston

Chronicles of Glenbuckle

CHRONICLES OF GLENBUCKIE

CHRONICLES

OF

GLENBUCKIE

BY

HENRY JOHNSTON

AUTHOR OF 'THE DAWSONS OF GLENARA,'
'MARTHA SPREULL,' ETC.

EDINBURGH: DAVID DOUGLAS
1889

CONTENTS.

PART FIRST.

CHAP.		PAGE
I.	GLENBUCKIE,	3
II.	THE REVEREND ROBERT M'WHINNIE,	14
III.	JAMIE PINKIE,—RADICAL,	32
IV.	THE MINISTER'S RECORD,	45

PART SECOND.

V.	MRS. M'WHINNIE, SEN., VISITS THE MANSE,	55
VI.	JAMES THOMSON OF THE GIRTLE,	64
VII.	ROBERT SIMPSON,	73
VIII.	THE MINISTER'S RECORD (*continued*),	84

PART THIRD.

IX.	TAMMAS SCOUGALL, THE MOLECATCHER,	97
X.	DR. GEBBIE,	112
XI.	MAGGIE WINLESTRAE,	126
XII.	THE MINISTER'S RECORD (*continued*),	137

CONTENTS.

PART FOURTH.

CHAP.		PAGE
XIII.	Jamie Pinkie makes a Proposal,	149
XIV.	Mysie Shaw, the Spaewife,	159
XV.	The Tempter,	169
XVI.	The Minister's Record (*continued*),	179

PART FIFTH.

XVII.	A Misunderstanding,	193
XVIII.	Polemical,	204
XIX.	Richie Neebikin's Courtship,	214
XX.	The Minister's Record (*continued*),	227

PART SIXTH.

XXI.	The Parish tries to make up its Mind,	239
XXII.	Peter Shule, the Betheral,	252
XXIII.	The Disruption,	264
XXIV.	The Minister's Record (*concluded*),	279

PART FIRST

CHAPTER I.

GLENBUCKIE.

It may be said in introducing these Chronicles that the characters depicted in them lived, moved, and had their being in a parish covering an area of less than twenty-five square miles. Glenbuckie may, however, be taken as typical of many other parishes in Scotland during the same eventful years. The period of time embraced is that between the passing of the Reform Bill in 1832 and the Disruption of the Church of Scotland in 1843.

Glenbuckie is situated in the county of Ayr—in that portion of it known as "Cunningham." The parish is bounded on the west by the sea, and on the east by a pleasant range of green hills. In the valley between these boundaries the village nestles snugly in surroundings of pastoral slopes and leafy shades. On the hillside above the village there is a substantial ruin, open to the elements, whose grey walls are laced with ivy, and freshened by an undergrowth of delicate lichens and ferns. Tradition points to this spot as the friendly refuge of Sir William Wallace, when his head was wanted by the southern king. The church and the manse occupy a platform of high ground half-way up the eastern slope, above and overlooking the village, a position not unsuitable for one charged with the moral and spiritual oversight of the people who live beneath. Here, also, is the parish burying-ground, with its ancient and irregular grave-stones, in which the male heads of families were wont to meet on Sundays before sermon-time, and discuss the prices of farm-stuffs, and talk over the latest aspect of political and ecclesiastical change. The village homes during the period of these Chronicles were of the plainest description—small thatched houses, with garden-plots behind—few of them possessing more accommodation than a simple "but and ben," and, in some cases, the "ben" had to afford accommodation for a loom. From the platform above, the minister, sitting in his study, on a calm day could hear the clack of the weaver's shuttle, and the clang of the cartwright's hammer—and, in the absence of these sounds, he might speculate as to the fresh moiety of intelligence that had reached the village, and was being turned over in the public mind. From this delightful eminence, looking out into the west, over the thin blue smoke of the village fires, one has a pleasant panoramic glimpse of sea and shore. In front there is a rocky headland, going sheer down for a hundred feet or so into the sea; but to right and left, as far as the eye can trace, may be seen long stretches of dazzling sand, on which the great foam-fringed waves are ever breaking, either with loving caress or in turbulent thunder. There are also brown roads skirting the beach, or meandering inland over fertile undulations, touching at picturesque farms, above which in summer weather the grey lark soars and sings. In the distance the rugged peaks of Arran and the dreamy hills of Bute rise out of the sea, and give pleasing irregularity to the skyline.

Though situated in convenient proximity to the sea, the natives of Glenbuckie were not a sea-faring people. Their wants were not extravagant, and these the district seemed to supply without any need on their part of engaging in the perilous and laborious occupation of going down to the sea in ships. Nanse Tannock, who kept the change-house at the east end of the village, where some of the post-coaches stopped to bait their horses, employed a couple of stout native lads as hostlers, besides a woman-of-all-work, and a maid to mind the dairy. Matha Spale, the cartwright, whose workshop occupied an open space at a place known as "The Cross," gave occupation to a man and two apprentice laddies. Beyond this there were only the domestic industries of tailoring, shoemaking, and weaving; it was therefore mainly in agricultural occupations that the people found employment. While absolute poverty was rarely known, the parishioners generally were of the very humblest class. This comparative poverty sprang not so much from the want of fairly lucrative occupation as from the idle habits engendered by the changeful and restless character of the times. Church and State needed mending—the latter, when reformed, would bring worldly prosperity, and the former would come in conveniently with comfort at the critical point when the State could afford no further aid. The people's zeal for political and ecclesiastical reform was greater than their ambition to improve the soil; indeed, many of those who occupied farms were ignorant of the first principles of agriculture and the laws on which these principles are based. While they were radicals so far as Church and State matters were concerned, they were strongly conservative in old methods of labour. Agricultural and other improvements were looked upon as dangerous innovations, and machinery of all kinds was held in superstitious awe. The winnowing-machine, or "fanners," as it was and is still called, had, it is true, been brought into the parish by Girtle of the Mains, a daring and a godless man, but it had been set down by his neighbours as an implement of the enemy, and was testified against as the "Deil's Wind," invented to overreach Nature and take the bread out of the mouths of honest families. The attention of the people, at the period of which these pages treat, was dangerously divided. The cracks of neighbours over march fences, and at village corners, together with the frequent meetings at Nanse Tannock's and the discussions that followed, were not conducive to the promotion either of peace or the advancement of worldly prosperity. To the more advanced spirits even the Reform Bill, when passed, was disappointing, inasmuch as they had still to work for their daily bread. Politics, however, sat lightly on the parochial mind in comparison with matters of ecclesiastical import. The spirit of uncompromising zeal, which led the founders of the Presbyterian Church to place but small store by their worldly possessions, was not wanting in Glenbuckie; for temporal prosperity was to them nothing compared with the inestimable blessing of spiritual independence!

Though the parish was now under the clement sway of the Rev. Robert M‘Whinnie, it had for many years previously been subject to the stern discipline of a different ruler. Under his predecessor, the Rev. Dr. Plunket, spiritual independence was a dead letter in so far as the exercise of private judgment was concerned. Inquiry was stifled, and absolute obedience was reckoned as an essential virtue. Was not he on the watch-tower? The wolves of heresy and schism, even in sheep's clothing, could be detected afar off by this lynx-eyed sentinel. It was his duty to watch and discriminate; it was theirs to follow and obey. This divine had seen many aspects of change in the Church. He had seen the Old Lights go out, and New Lights glimmer for a time above the ecclesiastical horizon; but, as he said, he never saw much good come of these mutations. He had kept his own house in order, while he himself clung loyally to the altar-horns of the Established Kirk.

Dr. Plunket was a firm disciplinarian. The smallest appearance of departure from time-honoured forms and customs was preached at from the pulpit, or dealt with privately by the session in no uncertain way. He was a faithful visitor at the homes of the people, and on these occasions he was never backward in "speerin' questions." By this means he acquired an intimate knowledge of their opinions, so far as they had any, and could readily detect anything like the semblance of declension in faith or manners. While this sternly consistent rule continued, the parishioners endured it with feelings of mingled respect and awe, but when a lighter rein fell on their necks, and the cry for spiritual freedom broke out over the land, what was to hinder them now as individuals from taking it up and echoing the demand to be delivered from Erastian bondage? Their previous period of enforced polemical inactivity had left them but poor subjects at argument. Ignorance assumed importance under the new feeling of liberty. Mere assertion in many cases took the place of logic, and any attempt by processes of reason to dislodge such disputants from their position generally ended in illogical irritation. The parishioner who, when sorely pressed by the arguments of a more enlightened disputant, replied, "Man, I canna argue wi' you, but I could fell ye," gave an answer fairly characteristic of his class.

In the ranks of the Church-reforming members of the parish there were simple, honest, self-denying, God-fearing men, whose search after truth was laborious if not profound. Their puzzlement and mental confusion in the presence of great moral and spiritual problems which it was not given them to comprehend, and their attempts at defining, in popular language, such questions as the "Rights of Conscience," the "Civil Magistrate," and the "Power of the Keys," furnish interesting psychological studies. Side by side with undoubted religious feeling there was much spurious piety. Long and compulsory study of the Westminster Standards, combined with an intimate knowledge of Scripture phrases, and the staid language of the old divines, had tended to give the speech, even of the common people, a somewhat sanctimonious tone. With many the use of this form of language, together with a meditative and morose manner of life, constituted the main evidences of godliness, and not unfrequently were such individuals found occupying ruling offices in the Church. Running through the political and religious enthusiasm of the period there was frequently found a full vein of grim and unconscious humour. Elements, often unimportant in themselves, were unduly magnified into essential principles, while main points in the controversy were as frequently left out of sight or passed by.

On this small stage also, the social and domestic virtues and vices of human character found suitable exponents. The green lanes under the manse brae, and the "lovers' loaning" leading to the shore, had been the scenes of many an uncouth and unrehearsed passage of love; here, as elsewhere, many passionate vows had been uttered which never reached fulfilment, resulting in bitter repentance, and sometimes, as will afterwards appear, in sorrowful and tragic shame. On long winter evenings the farmer's ingle would blaze with the cheery stack of peats, while neighbour lasses would bring their spinning-wheels to the "rocking," and the busy whirr of industry would mingle with the pleasant "daffing" of the lads. These meetings often awoke new feelings in the minds of both sexes—in the lasses' hope, and in the lads' desires—which not uncommonly resulted in secret visits to the bothie of Mysie Shaw, in order that the gipsy oracle, with her cantrip arts, might penetrate the future and declare what the upshot of it all would be. Mysie was the custodian of many a parish secret. Spinsters of ripe years had been known to reveal very illusory indications of amatoriness on the part of some desirable individual of the other sex, and appeal to her as to whether there was yet hope. Matrons had sought her help to win back the apparently declining affections of their guidmen, and it was said that an elder of the Kirk, who had lost a two-year-old quey, had invoked her aid, if peradventure he might recover his missing property. The spaewife, however, did not always wait to be sought out. She would sometimes convey admonishment or warning to those who did not seek her advice. She was no respecter of persons. In her mind there was no question of whether the recipient of her message was a believer in spae-craft or not. It was with her a matter of grim duty. Even the spiritual head of the parish had his secret failings reproved, and on one occasion it was said he received from her lips a fairly accurate forecast of the Disruption of the Kirk itself. Be that as it may, the inhabitants of Glenbuckie had not advanced sufficiently far into the century to be free from superstitious influences. When a child was born, the ancient matron in attendance took especial care to have it well washed in salt and water, and it was very important that the tiny creature should be made to taste the water thus mixed, three times, in order to preserve it from the influence of evil eyes. On such occasions there was always great anxiety felt until the bairn was christened. This feeling was fostered by the Confession, and also by the teaching of the Church in those days, as to the conditions under which salvation was possible in the case of infants. It was not uncommon to present children at the church for baptism when only two or three days old. It was looked upon as a dreadful risk to leave this duty long unperformed; for had not matrons of ripe years heard, on eerie nights, in the pauses of the storm, the piteous cries of unchristened bairns bewailing their hapless fate! Deaths seldom occurred, according to the shrewd gossips, without some remarkable "warning" being received of the sad event. The howling of a dog, the ticking of the death-watch, or some mysterious knock, was generally heard, either in the house of the person whose fate was portended, or in the dwelling of some relative or friend. There had often been, it was said, mysterious and awesome reappearances after death. The laird of Girtle had died, as was generally believed, a graceless man. Not being interested in Kirk affairs, he gave attention to the cultivation of his land, and made money. This money, by the strange irony of fate or fortune, had, after the death of his sister, which occurred subsequent to the Disruption, found its way into the treasury of the Free Church of Glenbuckie, and was the chief means of erecting the building in which the congregation worshipped. At this the spirit of the laird was manifestly perturbed, and it was said that the grave in the "auld kirkyard" had shown signs of disturbance about the time the Free Kirk building was finished; and on the testimony of soutar Wilson, who was held to be a fairly veracious man, while returning one Sunday night (quite sober, it was averred) from visiting a friend in Troon, the laird was distinctly seen by him occupying a proprietary position on the steeple, immediately below the vane. The appearance of the laird in this situation, as reported by soutar Wilson, was believed by some to be a solemn protest against the destination of his hard-earned savings, and particularly against the erection of a building which was not only extravagant in itself, but which gave painful indications of a return to the ornate and offensive architecture of the Church of Rome.

But it is unnecessary to prolong these introductory sentences. In the following pages the scenes and characters of Glenbuckie are sketched in ample detail; and it is hoped the reader will find in them a faithful record of events and feelings which agitated a Scottish parish during the earlier period of the present century.

CHAPTER II.

THE REVEREND ROBERT M'WHINNIE.

Nanse Tannock's change-house was a strange place for a meeting of the Glenbuckie session. It was, however, a festive occasion, for that day the Rev. Robert M'Whinnie was returning to his parish and people with a wife, whom he had newly wed. Robert Simpson had provided the first treat, the festival being on the voluntary principle. Robert was a tall, thin, jocose man, with an expressive face. When he laughed, his mouth played an important part in the performance, going well upwards on either side towards his ears, showing a fine double row of white teeth. It was a large, but not a vulgar mouth, evincing power—a mouth, in fact, of which a Demosthenes, ancient or modern, might have made noble use. Robert Simpson had a great capacity for humour, and his face was always an obedient mask of the mood he chose to adopt; indeed one never could tell beforehand whether it portended serious sentiment or extravagant humour.

"This is ae day o' our lives," said Simpson, closing

his lips firmly, and assuming a dramatic air. "To-day the minister o' Glenbuckie brings home a wife!"

"Hear, hear," cried Andrew Boles, a sturdy farmer known as Whinnyriggs, after the name of his farm.

"To-day we are met to do him honour," continued the speaker, "and to give them both the right hand o' fellowship. No doubt there are some disappointments at the minister going outside of the parish to find a wife, but that is no business of ours. It is an auld saying, 'One shall be taken, and another left'——"

"Canny wi' the Word, Robert," interrupted a grim-faced elder, who sat at the other end of the table, by name William Dickie.

"I mean no disrespect to the Word," said Robert. "A man canna marry twenty wives. The minister, like the rest o' us, has but one choice; and now that he has made his choice, it behoves us, as loyal sons o' the Kirk, to wish them joy; and this leads me to give you a toast—it is one you have maybe heard before, but it is none the waur o' that: 'May the hinges o' *friendship* never rust!'"

"Never rust," echoed numerous voices, as Simpson drained his glass and sat down. The sentiment he had just expressed was well known in the parish, but no one ever heard it without thinking of him. At convivial gatherings where Simpson was present he was sure to introduce it at some stage of the proceedings; but it invariably fell with a measure of freshness from his lips; for by his eccentricity of gesture, combined with his method of laying emphasis on different words, it always appeared to assume an aspect of novelty.

"It's no a bad toast," said soutar Wilson, smacking his lips after pledging it deeply, "and a guid dram o' Campbeltoun whisky is no a bad oil for keeping the hinges sweet.—Nanse, that's a drap o' grand drink."

"'Deed an' ye may say that," said the hostess, as she laid out the cakes and cheese on the table. "It ill becomes a Christian woman, let abee a lone widow body like me, to sell bad drink. There's no profit in it for either saul or body—for to hear the oaths and ill words that come oot o' simple folks' heads after drinking that coorse whisky is an affront to common decency."

"Nanse has spoken what is true," said William Dickie, when the oracle had withdrawn. "Swearin's very much to be deplored, and, as Nanse says, oaths come oot far owre handy when folk get a drap o' whisky."

"I'm thinkin'," said the soutar, speaking from the solid ground of a man who has a settled conviction on the point, "that the person who swears in drink maun have had the ill words rum'lin' aboot somewhere in his inside before he took it;

but for my pairt I canna see the sense o' swearin' ava, either in drink or oot o' drink."

"I'm no for saying again' a bit harmless aith," said Whinnyriggs, shaking his head in grave dubiety.

"An'rew Boles!" cried William Dickie, with several marks of exclamation in his voice, "I'm surprised to hear an elder o' the Kirk speaking in that licht wye. What does the Book tell ye? Does it not say—'Swear not at all'?"

"I admit that, William, but if I'm no mista'en, the Word means that mair as a veto again' rash vows than again' a bit sma', harmless, everyday aith. Man, when the coutar o' your pleugh takes a stane, and the shaft dings ye i' the ribs, or the stirks break through and mak' havoc o' the victual, as mine did the day, are ye no better to gie a bit damn and be dune wi't, than to glunch aboot a' day wi' the remembrance o' the thing sticking i' your throat? I appeal to the company if I'm no richt."

"There's common-sense in what you say," admitted the soutar.

"And logic," remarked Sandy M'Alpine warmly.

"Reason against Revelation," continued William Dickie, "the sinfu' heart against the Word o' Guid."

"The Word o' Guid canna be wrang," resumed M'Alpine in a puzzled way, "and a true logic argument should be square too. Dagont! I'm no saying but ye may be baith richt!"

"These are deep questions," interrupted Robert

Simpson, "deep questions o' theology and morals"—and Robert got to his feet. "We a' ken that William Dickie is a man o' wonderful religious insight—an expounder o' the law and the prophets; and that Whinnyriggs aye carries the licht o' day in his face, for he's nothing if he's no honest; but there, I would say, let the matter end. Let each man stand or fall by his own conscience. But we are no met to discuss the moral law—we are here for a different purpose."

"True, true!" piped Haplands, a farmer, whose surname was also the name of his farm.

Robert looked about him inquiringly, as if challenging dissent. "Weel," he continued, thumping the table with his clenched fist, "that being the case, why should we sit here argy-bargying like a presbytery of ministers? Fill your glasses to the brim for another toast." The speaker set the example, closed his lips firmly, and looked oracular. Was it to be a new accentuation of the "hinges of friendship," or a serious tribute to the newly wedded minister of Glenbuckie? The face was inscrutable. The mystery, however, remained unsolved, for, during the pause of preparing to do honour to the sentiment intended to be proposed, a heavy foot was heard hurrying to the door of the change-house.

"It's Richie Neebikin," exclaimed William Dickie (the name at one time had been Newbigging, but it had lost its identity in the mazes of a chequered descent). "They're surely no coming already." While they listened the door flew open with a bang, and a sturdy young fellow, with pink cheeks, knitted cap, and a great sleeved waistcoat, stood in the opening.

"Weel, Richie," said William Dickie, his master, "surely something pushes ye since ye have tint your manners. Is the minister coming?"

"Feggs, he's coming," replied the intruder, with sphinx-eyes riveted greedily upon the toothsome mounds of oat-cake and cheese. "I have ran till I'm barely fit to stand."

"Ay, ay, my man," said Simpson; "tak' up a piece o' bread and cheese, and tell us the news. Where did you see them?"

"Drivin'—roun'—the toll—on the Kilruskin road," said Richie, in the throes of mastication, "and by this time they maun be half-way up the Clincart Hill."

"Then we shouldna be here," said the soutar, seizing his hat. The messenger, with a supply of bread and cheese in each hand, was also retiring, when his master accosted him.

"Mind ye let aff the blunderbush just when they're passing the Mains. And—Richie——"

"Ay."

"If she should snap, ye ken, just put a fingerfu' o' poother i' the pan, and set lowe till 't wi' a bit o' match-paper—d' ye hear?"

Richie, however, did not hear, having taken to his heels in the excitement of the moment, in spite of his recent protestations of fatigue, with the view of being in time to give the minister and his wife the pre-arranged salute as the carriage passed the Mains.

Glenbuckie was in holiday attire that day. Almost every house displayed some evidence of welcome. Of course, there were seceders of various names in the parish, whose religious beliefs and forms of Church-government cut off their sympathies from the Established Kirk; but their number was few, so that the arrangements made gave the appearance of a general rejoicing. Flushed and excited by the dram and the importance of the occasion, the elders turned out and marched up the street towards the manse, headed by William Dickie and Robert Simpson. Robert, tall and erect, looked neither to right nor left, but gazed straight before him with bright twinkling eyes, and smiled an encouraging smile. William's whole exterior was a check upon levity. Even his umbrella, which he always carried when he wore his Sunday clothes, had a repressive look. From his face downwards —including a couple of legs which grew intimate about the knees, and from that point parted company as if their paths in life lay in different directions—he was a check upon light-heartedness of any kind. There was too much secular happiness in the world, and here was the man to keep it under solemn restraint by his controlling presence. So this strange procession marched up the village street, led on by the metaphorical embodiments of light and gloom.

One of the most elaborate of the many decorations displayed on the occasion was a sort of triumphal arch, extemporised by Matha Spale, the cartwright. Matha's workshop was situated in the centre of the village, about half-way between Nanse Tannock's change-house and the manse. Although the cartwright had no great knowledge of State or Church politics, he had some natural gifts of mechanical contrivance, which made him at least a useful member of society, and gave him authority in matters connected with his own craft. Matha, therefore, was not to be behind when the constructive faculty was called into operation. First he secured the consent and co-operation of Eneas M'Clymont, the blanket-weaver, whose loom-shop occupied the ground-floor of the house opposite. He then passed a rope from his own window to that of the weaver. This rope he propped high in the air by the aid of two poles, leaving sufficient room for the carriage to pass between. In the centre, and immediately above the carriage-way, was suspended a large orange-coloured banner, the lower corners of which were tied to the poles with scarlet cords, and bore this inscription :—

"These twain shall be one flesh—God bless them!"

There had been deep Bible and head searching over this part of the work, for, as the cartwright declared, "this supperscription had been the stiffest bit o' the hale business." Matha had at first proposed the simple phrase—"These twain shall be one flesh."

"Man, we maun have a motty wi' some sense in it," said the weaver, shaking his head, as he looked at his neighbour's proposal in black and white, feeling a sense of copartnery.

"Ay, but it 'll need to be Scriptural," replied the cartwright, shutting the Bible, which lay before him, with an irreverent snap. "I tell ye, I 'm sick and wearied o' the hale affair. If it was a common man, I could hit the nail on the head brawly—but a minister———." Matha thrust his fingers into his hair, placed his elbows on the arms of the chair, and looked dejectedly into the fire without finishing the sentence. The weaver read the phrase over again, turning the paper on which it was written in various ways, as if trying to look at the matter from all possible standpoints, then laying it down, he said—

"Weel, I 'll be hanged if I can see the sense o't ava!"

"But isn't it the very same wi' a heap o' Scripture?" queried the cartwright, raising an argumentative face. "Ministers can see a hantle farther into thae things than we can; it's their business, man. What would be the use o' them if things didna need explanation? I'll wager a groat the minister will think that supperscription fine."

"Would it no be better to say, 'Blessed is he that cometh in the name o' the Lord,' or something?"

"Tuts, that wouldna do ava. Don't ye see that leaves her oot a'thegither?"

"But so does the ither."

"Na, na, it touches them baith—'These twain.'"

"Ay, but what about the 'one flesh'? I dinna like that."

"Man, the 'one flesh' is grand."

"Dod, Matha, I canna see't. Div ye see't yoursel'?"

"I see it fine, if I could insense ye into it. Thae twa—that's the minister and his wife."

"Weel?"

"Weel, they're to be 'one flesh'—that means they're to be man and wife."

"I understand that, so far."

"But it means mair—far mair—if I could explain it to ye. Wha did ye weave your last wab o' blankets for?"

"For the wife at Whinnyriggs."

"Weel, what would ye have thocht when ye set out to tak' them hame, if the tae leg had said they're for Haplands, and the tither had said no, they're for Whinnyriggs. It would have been a bonnylike pliskie that; but nothing o' the kind happened: they were one flesh, baith o' the same mind, so they set aff peaceably thegither, and ye took the blankets hame. Dinna ye see it? The minister and his wife are like your twa legs, but if they are to be one flesh they maunna thraw wi' ane anither; they maun gang about the business o' life just as the members o' your body do, when you're weaving your blankets, or when you're taking them hame. Dod, man, it's a grand lesson."

"Weel, noo, when ye put it that wye it's no sae bad. Still-an-on, I would gie them a guid wish, or something."

"Weel, weel, let us say 'God bless them,' and be dune wi't." So the inscription ran—"These twain shall be one flesh—God bless them!"

The parish church was situated on a pleasant rising ground at the south end of the village. A rough wall enclosed the church and the graveyard which surrounded it, on three sides. Here

"The rude forefathers of the hamlet sleep."

The resting-places of these worthies were marked by stones of the most grotesque form and attitude. With perhaps one exception—a neat modern obelisk erected to the memory of the second son of the Earl of Killie—no builder's line ever seemed to have been applied to any of them. But the true perpendicularity of this modern monument only tended to show how deplorably far the others were out of plumb. A private avenue, lined with lilac and bourtree bushes, led from the churchyard to the manse. The house itself was a bulky square building, the front of which was profusely laced with ivy. The elders, already arrived, had taken up positions on either side of the porch.

Mrs. Janet Pyat, the ancient housekeeper, stood in the door, shading her eyes with a wrinkled hand, sternly surveying a neighbouring height, on which a small knot of villagers were actively engaged in some new ploy which she apparently could not make out.

"What's yon they're doing on Drumsynie Hill?" inquired Mrs. Pyat.

"They're erecting an altar to the Dadians," replied Robert Simpson unblushingly.

"To the wha?" demanded the housekeeper with stern emphasis.

"The Dadians are the spirits o' mirth and frolic; some think they are related to the Crackanalians, and others to the Nickadumphians, but I never could see they were connected with either." Simpson had a mythology of his own, and for the moment he certainly was under the influence of his favourite deities—the Dadians.

"Who ever heard the like o' that? Robert Simpson, do you believe what ye say?"

"It's only Robert's wye o' saying that the callants are bigging a bonfire," explained William Dickie soothingly.

"I ask Robert Simpson if he believes what he says," said Mrs. Pyat, ignoring William Dickie's pacific interruption.

"To be sure," replied Robert, stepping forward to meet the attack. "Surely you havena lived a' the days o' your life in a minister's family without believing in sperits, Janet Pyat?"

"I have read my Bible weel, Robert, and I have listened wi' edification to the sainted Dr. Plunket's sermons for twenty years, and never heard mention o' ony sic sperits, and if they're no in the Bible, and no kent by the godly minister that's awa', I'm thinking they shouldna be found in the mouth of an elder o' the Kirk o' Scotland."

"True," said Whinnyriggs, screening the merry twinkle of his eyes by the use of a red pocket-handkerchief. "You have had great opportunities, Mrs. Pyat, and by this time ye should ken a' the sperits that are worth kenning by name."

"I make no pretence, Whinnyriggs, no pretence ava, but I canna allow sic idle words as Robert Simpson has used to pass without raising my solemn testimony against them. There are owre mony whigmaleeries and nonsense in folk's head noo-a-days."

"'Deed ay," said William Dickie seriously; "it'll

take us a' to be eidently on the watch-tower to protect the doctrines o' the Kirk. There's owre muckle speritual independence, and an evil proneness to divisive courses, that maun be held in check."

"Mrs. Pyat," said Simpson, looking down on his colloquist with calm magnanimity, "I'm no here to defend either the Crackanalians or the Nickadumphians, for I don't like either o' them. From what I can learn, they are the representatives o' envy, intolerance, bigotry, and persecution, but I aye upheld the Dadians; no man or woman either ever heard me speak ill o' them, for whatever may be said o' the others, I canna but allow that the Dadians are the boys."

The conversation was interrupted by movements which clearly betokened that the bridal party was at hand. The lads on Drumsynie had just unfurled a great red flag above the combustible cairn raised by them on the uppermost shoulder of the hill. This was followed by the sharp, rattling noise of wheels, accompanied by rounds of lusty cheering from the narrow thoroughfare below, and it became known to the elders that there was no time to lose in placing themselves at the door in order to receive the Rev. Robert M'Whinnie and his bride.

"What's come owre that numskull, Richie Neebikin?" said William Dickie testily; "the sorrow should have set off that blunderbush five minutes syne."

"I ettle the gun's no often in use," ventured Haplands.

"Only on great occasions. It was first used by my grandfather against Dundee in the battle o' Loudon Hill, and it was last fired at the ordination o' the late lamented Dr. Plunket when he cam' to Glenbuckie parish—ye see it's a religious gun."

"Religious or no religious," said Andrew Boles, "it's a mercy the auld-farrant thing didna gang off and blaw oot somebody's brains." As Whinnyriggs spoke, the steaming horse emerged from the bourtree bushes, and in a few seconds drew up in front of the manse door.

As the minister assisted his wife from the carriage William Dickie cleared his throat, and stretching out his hand gravely, said—

"As senior elder o' this parish, sir, I offer ye the right hand o' fellowship, and wis' ye much joy in the holy bands o' wedlock; and you, mem," he continued, turning to the blushing girl-wife, who stood looking wonderingly on, "you're welcome to Glenbuckie. I hope ye'll be long spared to uphold the hands and strengthen the heart o' our respected pastor, and that ye may gang in and out amongst us as an ensample to the flock."

"There's no fear o' her," said the redoubtable Mrs. Pyat, who kept the door while the elders one by one offered the right hand of fellowship to the minister. "There's no fear o' her, so lang as she gives the go-by to the Episcolaupians and the Romans, for, as the godly Dr. Plunket used to say——"

"Janet," said the minister,—"Janet, will you have the goodness to show Mrs. M'Whinnie to her room?"

"Rebuff number one," thought Mrs. Pyat, fingering the long, well-starched ties of her high-backed white cap. "He's had the first fling, but we'll see who will have the last." With this reflection she tossed her head in the air significantly, and led the way into the house.

"Brethren," said Mr. M'Whinnie, turning to the elders as his wife left them, "after the fatigues of your own kind preparations and of our journey, I feel sure you will excuse, or as I might otherwise express it, pardon me if I simply, and in a word, thank you in name of Mrs. M'Whinnie and myself for your loyal and hearty reception. Nevertheless, although my wife is a total abstainer, and hopes to disseminate her principles in the parish, I cannot, for the present, allow you to separate without asking you ben to have a dram."

The minister led the way into his study, and bringing out a well-filled decanter, helped his elders to the hospitalities of the manse.

"Robert Simpson," said Whinnyriggs, "we'll tak' the word from you."

Simpson stood for a second or two with his lips firmly set, looking thoughtfully into his glass.

"Brethren o' the session," he said slowly,

"Whinnyriggs has asked me to be your mouthpiece in proposing the health o' our minister and his bonny bride. I consider it a high honour and a privilege to be here to receive you, sir, and to be permitted to drink to your health and to the health o' the lady you have just brought home. In these days o' division and secession it is our duty to be loyal to the principles o' the Established Kirk, and to strengthen the hands o' those who minister in her sacred offices. It is our duty to suffer wi' you in your trials, and to rejoice wi' you in your happiness, as we do this day. It is well said that a guid wife is a crown to her husband, but I will say this, that if your wife is half as guid as she is bonny, ye'll be happier than the best crowned head in the land. I wish you both much happiness——" Robert paused and looked inquiringly round, then he added with an unexpected and vigorous snap, "and—may the *hinges* of friendship never rust!"

Although some of the elders, and especially William Dickie, felt somewhat scandalised at this familiar, and, as they thought, too secular sentiment being incorporated with so solemn a duty, they nevertheless passed the matter over in silence, and, nodding respectfully to the minister, took off their dram.

Haplands, however, who had received instructions before leaving home to be sure and drink the minister's health wise-like, and no stand gaping like a "silly sumph" and allow everybody else to do the "crackin'," took advantage of the pause and said, "Here's to your health, sir, and your mistress's too, and I am sure me and my mistress wishes ye baith weel." At the conclusion of these remarks the speaker, anxious to make up with the others, took his whisky rather hurriedly, resulting in an explosion which forced him into inglorious retirement.

"What was yon he said about his wife's principles?" said Whinnyriggs, as the elders wended their way through the churchyard towards the village.

"Gore! and didna I notice that too!" exclaimed M'Alpine, his face beaming with the realisation of his own astuteness. "He used a guid wheen words about his wife yonder I didna like ava."

"An abstainer, or something, he ca'd her," said Haplands; "I hope he hasna brought hame a woman o' a different persuasion frae himsel'."

"Thae English," remarked the soutar, "as Janet Pyat weel kens, are either Romans or Episcolaupians, and there's no saying."

CHAPTER III.

JAMIE PINKIE, RADICAL.

The wave of agitation which swept over the country previous to the passing of the first Reform Bill did not fail to penetrate even into Glenbuckie. The interests of land and labour were as keenly discussed here as they were in other parts of the country. The farmers, though at heart desirous of reform, had too much at stake to take any prominent part in the agitation to bring it about. It is true the Earl of Killie did not himself attempt to interfere with the rights and opinions of his tenants; but they were sufficiently held in hand by his fussy factor, Mr. Cunningham, who was a keen partisan on the Tory side. The clergy, under the influence of patronage, doubting, as many of them did, the wisdom of placing too much power in the hands of the people, either kept out of the arena of politics altogether, or denounced the Reform Bill as a dangerous measure—so that the agitation in Glenbuckie was mainly confined to the irresponsible, or labouring classes.

James Pinkerton—or Jamie Pinkie, as he was commonly called—was perhaps the most active politician in the county. Jamie was poor from various causes. He was a tailor to trade; exceedingly fond of a dram, and ever ready to join the smith, the blanket-weaver or any other drouthie cronie in discussing the malpractices of crowned heads, statesmen, and others whose interests seemed to him to stand in the way of realising the glorious principles of "The Rights of Man." Jamie was born to rule, not to work, but his kingdom as yet was not large. From his lowly position he had nothing to risk, but everything to gain, by the extreme views he entertained; his followers were therefore mainly of his own class. There was one faithful believer who supported his throne—or, to be more accurate, platform, for he hated thrones—and shared his poverty—that was his sister Jean. The confidence which she placed in his power of statecraft, and the appreciation he entertained for her discrimination and sympathy, made them helpful to each other. This sympathy had developed by frequent exercise, for her brother had met with many disappointments. In spite of the gnawing pinch of want, and the galling misrule of kings and governments, Jamie had had some pleasant dreams. The radical period which succeeded the battle of Waterloo, embraced one of these. Jamie had been chosen one of the delegates to represent Ayrshire on the Glasgow

Executive, which was the chief council of the movement. He had made frequent journeys to that important capital of the cause, and delivered himself of much vigorous, if rough eloquence, under the roof of the favourite radical houff—The Boar's Head in the Old Wynd. Jamie's theory was to co-operate with his English compatriots until they had abolished monarchy, but when that was accomplished, he held that the two countries should be governed by separate executives; that the land should be apportioned equally amongst the people; that the counties should be of a uniform size; and that each should appoint a member to represent it in the management of the affairs of state. Jamie had already settled in his own mind what part of the lands of Cunningham, in his native county, should fall to him.

"The land o' the coney, Jean," her brother would say, rubbing his hands in gleeful anticipation. "Dod, it's weel named, for there's no a place in a' the country like it for rabbits. Ye'll never want for rabbit soup, my lass, a dainty ye're partial to; and as for that meadow field o' William Dickie's— a bushel o' guid tawtie seed, planted early i' the spring, in ae corner o't, will keep ye frae want during the six or seven months i' the year I may be absent frae ye in the Embro' parliament."

"But," said his sister, casting a timid glance of admiration at the valiant little member of parliament to be—" when ye gang to Embro'——"

"Stuff and nonsense, Jean! I ken fine what ye're gaun to say. I have telt ye mony a time before that I'll never marry. We have been thegither noo for a guid wheen years, and I tell ye plainly, I micht get waur than you—a guid heap waur. A man kens wha he has, but he disna ken wha he may get. Noo, I'll tell ye a secret that I never breathed in mortal ear before, and let it comfort ye. The thing happened the last time I was at Glasca. We had had a long seat in the Boar's Head hearing reports frae the delegates—that was the nicht I had the waup at Jock M'Cunn, the mad twister chap frae the Calton, that I telt ye aboot. Weel, after I had settled Jock M'Cunn, Bailie Macannel, the chandler in the Gallowgate, would have me doon to his house, and I was nane loath, for to tell ye the truth, Jean, I was baith hungry and dry. The Bailie and I finished twa gills, while his daughter was toasting the Welsh rabbit. Weel, ye ken, if onything gars me eat it's Welsh rabbits, and the wye that lassie toasted them, and turned them, and peppered them, and better peppered them, fairly took my head, and when she served them up pipin' hot, as broon as a bervie, while we were in the middle o' our third gill, I could have ta'en her in my arms and proposed to her clean aff-hand."

"Oh, Jamie!"

"It's true, perfect true. Dod, Jean, ye never saw sic handling o' a Welsh rabbit; but mark what

I did, noo, just mark what I did. Reason said—Jamie, wait till the morn; ye're a great politician, and a politician should never do anything in a hurry; ye have a decent kind o' sister at hame, and though she canna mak' Welsh rabbits like Miss Macannel, she has stuck by ye, and believed in ye, and noo that ye're gaun to Embro' as a representative in the new parliament, I appeal to ye, Jamie, is it fair?

"Dod! it was a hard struggle, Jean, it was a hard struggle, I can tell ye, for she was a bonnie lassie besides; but I just said to myself—Jamie, ye maunna gi'e in either to beauty or Welsh rabbits the noo; so I slept owre it, and here I am. Jean, ye have reason on yer side: and though women-folk ken little about reason, it is fortunate for you that she exercises a great influence among men."

Having now once for all settled this delicate question, he must needs turn his attention to matters of higher import. "William Dickie must go," he continued after a profound pause, "I'm determined on that. I'll put up a castle o' four rooms and kitchen on the knowe, abune whaur his barn at present stands; and do ye ken what we'll ca' it, Jean? We'll ca' it Bodkin's Castle. It'll be a glorious thing to sit there i' the lull o' parliamentary business, in sicht o' the sea and the Arran hills, an' work oot the great problem o' political reconstruction. Ye can sit up there beside me if ye like, and do the shewin', for there'll be nae mair shewin' for me then, though, I daursay, there 'll be a heap o' parliamentary darnin' to do after the holes we 'll mak' i' the Constitution."

"But are you fairly set on turning William Dickie oot o' his place?" inquired his sister seriously.

"Buttons and buttonholes, stump and branches; ye ken the pairt William Dickie played wi' Dr. Plunkit, in cuttin' me aff frae the Kirk. The Kirk is just a tool i' the hands o' Government for striking at the root o' reform. Every dog has its day, and Dr. Plunkit and William Dickie have had theirs— so William maun gang to the wa'. I dinna ken what we may do wi' the Colonies, Jean; that's an important question for the new Parliament. I think it would be a guid thing to banish the ministers to ane o' them—maybe Canada or New Zealand—whaur they could preach to ane anither. I'm thinkin' it would settle a wheen o' them—they ken owre muckle o' each ither to stand that—they would be driven to work for their bread like ither folk. As to William Dickie, if he cares to bide at hame, we'll gi'e him a bit o' grund somewhere, but it must be *ex gratia*, Jean, entirely *ex gratia*—of course you canna be expected to ken what that means—it's i' the classic language; but it's a gran' phrase, and signifies, purely oot o' peety. And if ever he says *Corn Laws* again abune his breath, he's a ruined man."

At this point, Eneas M'Clymont, the blanket-weaver, came in with great news. "Birmingham and Manchester are up in airms," he cried. "Twa hundred thousand Reformers are in the field. Major Cartwright, Sir Charles Wolseley, and Mr. Hunt, have ta'en the command, and what do you think?—ane o' the standards they have carried into the field bears a likeness o' Sir William Wallace, wi' this motty under it—'God armeth the patriarch.'"

"The patriot, M'Clymont, the patriot," said Jamie, speaking demonstratively under a feeling of mortification, that he, a delegate, should receive in the presence of his sister, such important information from a blanket-weaver. "But whaur got ye sic news?"

"Frae the chapman," said M'Clymont, submitting humbly to the correction. "He has just come frae Kilmarnock, whaur the news is in everybody's mouth, an' he's e'en noo in Nanse Tannock's back kitchen sellin' his wares for next to nothing, as he says he is gaun to gie up the pack, and tak' to the poother and pike business, wholesale."

"Birmingham and Manchester are to seize London," said Jamie, putting his finger to his forehead and speaking dramatically, "while a' north o' the Tweed are to strike a fell blow at Embro'. Dod! M'Clymont, this is great news; Jean, I maun gang doon to Nanse Tannock's withoot delay; no doot the packman has private papers for me, an' if he has, every moment is worth a lapful o' goud. Cheer up, Jean, lass, dinna worry yoursel' aboot the Welsh rabbits. My word! if this English business be true, Bodkin Castle is as sure as death."

The story, however, was not true as related by M'Clymont. A meeting had been held at Birmingham on the 12th July 1819; it was computed that 15,000 persons were present, and at this meeting Major Cartwright and Sir Charles Wolseley were elected to represent the people of Birmingham in Parliament. In the following month a great meeting was held in Manchester for the purpose of petitioning for Reform in the House of Commons. The various bodies represented at this meeting were accompanied by bands of music, and carried banners on which were inscribed various mottoes and devices, amongst them the motto which M'Clymont had quoted so grotesquely. This gathering numbered upwards of 80,000 persons. Mr. Hunt was the principal speaker, but a body of yeomanry coming suddenly upon the scene the crowd was unceremoniously dispersed, and Hunt was seized and carried off to prison.

These disappointments were galling to the ardent spirit of our reformer; but it was not until the ill-concerted radical rising, which terminated in the farce enacted at Bonnymuir, near Stirling, that Jamie began to perceive the futility of attempting to realise their hopes on the lines which he and other extravagant revolutionists like himself had laid down.

Though these events had left him wiser, they by no means made him a soberer man. Reforms had been promised of a constitutional character, but as none of them embraced Bodkin Castle, or held out the hope of an Edinburgh Parliament, they could only be viewed as temporising measures which, while they might satisfy some, could not afford the people that degree of justice which the stern radical programme demanded. Jamie was a more frequent visitor at Nanse Tannock's since the discontinuance of the executive meetings in Glasgow. Such eloquence as his would not willingly hide itself under a bushel. His sister was a patient and sympathetic listener, but, as he said afterwards (the occasion being one of the sederunts in the village change-house), "It is dry and profitless work talking to a woman—women may conceive and bring forth heroes, but it is the province o' men to shape and put in operation the great forces that are destined to regenerate the world."

Eneas M'Clymont cried "hear, hear," and filled up his glass at Matha Spale's expense, in honour of this robust sentiment.

"Man, Jamie, it's a terrible peety that Embro' Parliament affair o' yours fell through," said Whinnyriggs, removing his pipe and trying to square his face. "It would have been a better job for ye than this miserable needle and thumble business. I'll no say but they micht hae made ye Prime Minister."

"He would have made a Prime Minister," said Richie Neebikin, having but an imperfect apprehension of what was meant by this phrase. "Just think o' what routh o' talk he has. Losh! hoo he would hae skelpit us through the commandments. Jamie, what would ye mak o' the Chief end o' Man?"

"That question may be speered in jest or in ignorance," Jamie remarked solemnly, "but it has mair in it that ever entered into Richie Neebikin's head to think o'. I can tell ye it's a great subject, that 'Chief end o' Man,' and I'll no say but the Question Book gies a fair enough answer till 't in a broad and general way; but the subject has a political as weel as a moral side. Is it glorifying to the Almichty to let the tyrant rule, and red-handed injustice ride wat-shod owre the necks o' the puir? When the deevil has got abroad and put the whole body politic out o' joint, is it glorifying to the Almichty to sit still and sing Psalms o' peace and contentment as if there were no wrongs to right and no crying acts o' injustice to redress? Is that patriotism? What would Wallace or Bruce or John Knox think o' ye—tell me that? Would *they* be hauden doon by kings or governments, or the irksome tyranny of priestcraft? Puir, puir Scotland! I fear yer sons noo-a-days have but a miserable notion o' the Chief end o' Man."

Jamie leant forward and gazed with disgust into the empty gill stoup on the table before him, looking as if they had now reached the lowest depths of patriotic poverty.

"I agree for the maist part wi' what ye say, Jamie," said Davit Wilson the soutar; "but, man, what's the use o' solitary individuals knockin' their noses off against established preenciples? Things have ta'en a lang while to grow into their present shape, an' ye canna alter the growth o' years in a day. It's a question o' time."

"T-i-m-e!" retorted the tailor, repeating the word with derisive emphasis. "I tell ye, Davit, it's a matter o' immediate pike-staffs and guns; and if the people winna tak' that plan it will be a question o' eternity. Look at the French!"

"And what have they made o't?" inquired the soutar.

"They can turn society upside doon pretty smairt," retorted Jamie gleefully.

"Ay, ay, and then they dinna rest till the doonside is bunemost again. Man, the French are just like a wheen puir puddocks, aye loup loupin', and they nae sooner get on a bit o' dacent dry grun' than they sprachle back again into the mud. I can tell ye, Jamie, however keen I may be for reform, I'm no in wi' the French."

"It's my opinion we'll get all we want by-and-by," said Whinnyriggs; "the folk abune us are beginnin' to see that things are no just square. It's a' nonsense to talk o' pikes an' guns when there are weel-fed sodgers to face. Ye may tak' my word for 't, Jamie; radical bluid is far owre thin to do much guid to the country."

"Faith, I dinna like the skailin' o' bluid," remarked M'Alpine, rubbing a full-orbed and contemplative face. "I wouldna say again' a body o' men takin' pikes and guns, and maybe gieing a bit roar or twa owre the hill just to fricht the government, if that would bring aboot better times; but, dagont! if they saw that wouldna do, they should tak' to their heels an' rin!"

The tailor looked disgusted beyond expression with this sentiment. He tried the gill-stoup again, but it was empty of all consolation. Had M'Alpine been capable of making a joke, Jamie would gladly have treated his remarks as such, but it was well known that conscious humour was not a trait in his character. As a good-natured well-to-do farmer, who was not loath to give a dram to any needy friend or neighbour afflicted with thirst, Jamie could tolerate him; but as a politician and a patriot—well, it is needless to record the tailor's opinion. Jamie might have opened a full battery of scathing invective upon the unpatriotic head, had not expediency prompted silence, for there was no man in the company more likely than M'Alpine to refill the measure on the table which had now stood so long and so hopelessly empty.

"I doot, Jamie, ye have got a stitch i' yer inside," said Whinnyriggs, watching the play of mixed feelings on the tailor's face as the laugh subsided. "Are ye ill?"

Jamie replied with a groan. "No," he said, "but I'm *dry*. M'Alpine's jokes should aye be followed by a guid sup o' whisky to wash them doon."

CHAPTER IV.

THE MINISTER'S RECORD.

As the Lord knoweth it has long been my intention to take note in written form of my thoughts and doings, not that I have any vainglorious hope that the world will care much about what I think or do, but because I believe it will be most useful and edifying to myself; for one cannot do an evil thing, or think an evil thought, without pondering over it with sadness of heart when he comes to write it down, and in this way I entertain the hope that this record will be a deterrent to hasty or unholy thoughts and actions, while it will serve as a great spur to maintain a virtuous and becoming walk in life. What could be more opportune than to begin this record from the date of one's marriage, for verily the whole course of one's life gets changed, or at least greatly modified thereby. The marriage state is truly a great novelty, especially to one who enters it so late in life. It is my earnest prayer that I may not be tempted to linger too passionately over its delights at the expense of duty; but surely the Great

Disposer of events, who instituted this holy state, cannot be wroth with His children for pausing fondly over one's early nuptial joys. To me everything seems changed—even the manse itself has a different air, or, I may say, aspect, since my dear wife entered it. Such mutations as have taken place are not well-pleasing to poor Mrs. Pyat, who is without doubt, as my wife says, a person of the old school. To find a withdrawing-room above my study, in a place which used to be filled with boxes and old lumber, with a musical instrument in one corner, and a grand couch and other articles of luxury and adornment tastefully arranged in it, is to me very wonderful, and seems like the realisation of some fairy dream. Such a change, too, in my study! The confusion of years has now fallen into a state of order, so much so that I do not seem half so rich in books as I was constrained to believe; indeed the rearrangement is so complete that it is impossible for me to lay hands on any book I may want without hours of diligent search. But I know it is all for the best, and doubtless I shall get used to this supreme state of orderliness in due time.

I went through the parish to-day, and it was heartsome and cheering to receive, as I did, the earnest congratulations of my faithful people. William Dickie accompanied me as far as Girtle Mains, but on account of the infirmity in his nether limbs, he was unable to go further, and truly it was just as well, for poor Girtle, who is in failing health, used language about William which it would not have been edifying for him to hear, and which indeed was far from Christian in its character or tone. William Dickie has a zeal not always conjoined with prudence, or as I might otherwise designate it, judgment, which at times gives offence. For all that, he is a man of stern piety, and it pained me exceedingly to hear him abused.

Nevertheless my perambulations were not without pleasure, for it was gratifying to observe that some important and satisfactory improvements have been effected during my brief absence, or at least since my last visitation. William Dickie has now got a new gate that opens to your hand with great sweetness. The factor has also caused the barn at Haplands, which was so sadly out of order, to be put in decent repair, and has put slates on the dwelling-house where the thatch was before, so that the place has quite a snod and canty look. The mistress, however, is a very masterful woman, and has an outspoken tongue. I fear her husband, as an elder of the Kirk, is not so discreet as one could wish, and may have disclosed some doings of the session which it was not meet for him to make known. For, what did she do but take me in task for our dealings with that poor, silly lassie Maggie Winlestrae, whose case was before us at last meeting, and gave me question and answer, as near as may be, showing that she was fully cognisant of what had passed. But that was not all, for she would not be hindered from believing, and saying to my face, that my wife was unsound in the faith. She said I must not blame her, as the same thing was believed by members of my own session. She is truly a bold, ignorant, and senseless woman, who thinks everything becomes her, and it required great Christian restraint and patience to answer her with dignified calmness. After what I told her, however, I opine the slander will go no further, for it would be very detrimental to my wife's influence if such stories were allowed to be bruited over the parish without contradiction. I suspect Mrs. Pyat, who has shown some jealousy of her youthful mistress, has had something to do with the matter, but I must take time and inquire thereinto with prudence and temperate consideration.

It is curious how our joys are mixed up, or as one may say, interwoven with incidents that give us pain, but no doubt these things are from the hand of an all-wise Providence, and are intended to remind us that perfect and sustained felicity is not intended to be our lot on this side of the grave. The incident which suggested this reflection occurred in this wise: I had just passed along the head rigg of the clover-field at the Mains march, and was stepping over the stone dyke into the loaning, when who should stand up before me but that strange gipsy-woman, May Shaw, well known as "Spae Mysie." Her appearance was so unexpected and her manner so strange that I got an uncommon fright. Nevertheless I found courage to address her: I saw she had something to say to me and I deemed it better to have the first word. My remark was about the weather, for to tell the truth I did not know what else to say. But she put the remark aside without ceremony, and said it did not matter much when she and I were under the yird what kind of weather we had to-day. It was a true saying, but not a very happy one to a person who had so recently entered into the joys of wedlock, and who was looking forward to a protracted period of useful and happy labour.

"May," I said seriously, "I hope it is well with you."

"Never fash wi' me," she replied; "weel or ill mak's little differs to Mysie. The ill is geyan often bunemost; but that's neither here nor there."

I thought the poor natural, her son, whom she loved so tenderly, was maybe ailing, but my inquiries regarding him were also set aside bluntly.

"I want to know, is it right wi' yoursel'?" she said. "Ministers should practise as weel as preach. There is an auld remark in the Question Book that I hinna forgotten, where we are tauld to honour our father and mother that our days may be long in the land. Was your mother, puir body, no guid enough to be invited to her ain son's wedding?"

The question, I admit, had been borne in on my conscience before, and this observe was like a red-hot iron going still nearer to the quick. I was overwhelmed for the moment, and had no mind left to reply, but she went on without waiting.

"Oh, it is a sore thing to be a mother and find that those we have nursed on our breast, and toiled for, are ashamed o' us after we have worn out our best days to make them better than ourselves. She was not fit company for your bonny bride and her braw relations. The pleasures o' the marriage-board would have been marred by homely wisdom and Doric speech. No wonder the bride resolved that her present to the lowly dame should be a stuff-gown—silk was owre guid to draigle on an earthen floor."

"May," I said, "May, surely some one has told you——"

"The truth," she interrupted; "maybe it is painful for you to hear, as it is for me to tell." She paused, looked reflectively on the ground, sighed as if moved with the thought of similar neglect in some far-off time. "It is no doubt the way of the world, and maybe the world will justify its own ways. Far be it from puir Mysie to preach to the minister of Glenbuckie, but she has said what was on her mind, and richt or wrang ye maun leeze out the tangled hank for yoursel'." In a moment this weird oracle had stepped over amongst the tall whin-bushes and disappeared. I confess my mind was sore troubled. The hank she had left me to unleeze was truly a tangled one. My mother lived thirty miles from Glenbuckie, my marriage had taken place in Glasgow, and how could this strange creature know what she had just disclosed? Some said she had the second sight, and knew wonderful secrets by the turning of cups and other uncanny cantrips, but this I can hardly believe. At any rate she is an awsome creature, and her words have worked me sore uneasiness, for try as I like I cannot get them out of my head.

There is another matter which gives me some concernment in my moments of reflection, and that is my wife's views on what she calls the total abstinence question—that is, total abstinence from alcoholic liquors. It is true, no doubt, that excessive drinking is injurious to the public weal, but those who are used to taking their dram in moderation I fear will not brook such new-fangled interference. William Dickie shook his head gravely when I spoke of the matter to-day. He is afraid of innovations. "One thing leads on to another," he said, "and change of habits might lead to divers changes in matters of belief, and it would be better to let well-enough alone."

I have much faith, however, in my wife's prudence, especially when she gets to know the kittle nature of the ground on which she stands. Her previous training has been in large centres of population, where the vice of intemperance comes more painfully into view, but as she gets better acquainted with our staid and fixed habits she will probably be more inclined to modify her opinions.

I regret to state that after meeting the spaewoman my mind was in such a state of ferment, or as I may say perturbation, that I was totally unable to visit Thomas Tangle, the forester's son, who got himself so badly burnt at the tar-barrel accident that night of the rejoicings at our home-coming. For this and other sins of omission and commission I hope to obtain forgiveness, but, God willing, I will overtake this duty early on the morrow, for in sooth the lad's limbs have been sorely bitten by the cruel flames.

PART SECOND

CHAPTER V.

MRS. M'WHINNIE, SENIOR, VISITS THE MANSE.

LIKE many of the Scottish clergy, the Rev. Robert M'Whinnie was born of very humble parents. It was not an uncommon thing for families of the class to which he belonged, to set aside one of their male members for the Church; and this was too often done without much thought as to the child's capacity or adaptation for the work. There was something heroic, however, in this devotion, because when the family was very poor, it involved considerable hardship and self-abnegation on the part of every other member of it, in order to keep and pay the expenses of one of their number while going through the long years of educational preparation previous to his "getting a kirk." It was said that the senior Robert M'Whinnie had been a miner in Lanarkshire, and that his son had himself served some time, early in life, as a draw-boy in a coal mine; but this, if true, is not to the discredit either of his family or himself. There was one thing, however, which had puzzled some inquisitive and meddlesome people in the parish, and that was the almost total absence of his relatives from the manse. His mother, who was now a widow, had, it was said, not once looked near the place during the five years of his ministry. And Mrs. Pyat said she could count on her five fingers all the visits his brothers and sisters had paid in that time. In fact, she "didna wonder at the minister no encouraging them about the place, for the brothers would smoke black cutty pipes a' through the house; and the sisters were never happy anywhere but in the kitchen, where they were to be found palavering with the servant woman and keeping her off her work." However it came about, whether from ignorant pride on the one side or from false shame on the other, there was the absence of that generous family sympathy which ought to have existed, and which probably would have existed had Robert been allowed in his earlier years to remain at home and work for his own bread. Cynics have made the remark that, while ministers look to the next world for their reward, they have an objection to be straitened or pinched in their circumstances here. Hence the frequent association of their matrimonial views with money. The Rev. Robert M'Whinnie could not be said, so far as his marriage was concerned, to belong to this class. It was late in life before he got settled in a charge, and though he had viewed fair maidens with amorous eyes, and, it was hinted, proposed to not a few, he remained wifeless for some time after his induction to the pastorate of Glenbuckie. His time, however, came. At a synod meeting in Glasgow he was introduced to a young lady of good family, but little fortune, who, rumour said, was suffering at the time from the sting of disappointment in a love affair, the upshot of which was the matrimonial alliance referred to in an earlier chapter of these Chronicles. No members of the M'Whinnie family were present at the ceremony. They, and their ministerial relative had, in the process of time, drifted so far apart that, perhaps, it would not have been a kindness to have brought them into contact with new relatives whose habits and social status were so different from their own. It had been arranged, however, between the minister and his wife, so soon as they were comfortably settled in the manse, that Mrs. M'Whinnie, senior, should be invited to visit them and offer her congratulations. Accompanying the invitation the young wife had sent her mother-in-law the "stuff gown" referred to by the spae-wife, a present which in the circumstances was considered to be more serviceable than one of costlier material.

The elder Mrs. M'Whinnie came on by the Dumfries coach due at Glenbuckie about five o'clock in the afternoon. She had not taken thought or trouble to write that she was coming, but all the same she was deeply, though unreasonably offended, that "Robin" had not come down to meet her. She called at Nanse Tannock's to inquire the way to the manse, and on getting directions took care to tell that personage the relationship in which she stood to its occupants.

"Indeed, mem," said Nanse, dropping a courtesy.

"Ye needna 'mem' me," replied Mrs. M'Whinnie, who was rather a blunt person. "I'm a common body like yoursel', and no muckle used to becking and bowing. I have just come aff the coach, and expected my son to meet me."

"'Deed, and it's a cauld seat at the best," said Nanse, "and especially so on a hairst day, wi' the mist lying thick i' the glen. Ye'll be nain the waur o' a drap o' sperits to put life into ye."

"No ae bit, mistress; it's very kind o' ye to think o't, I'm sure."

"I shouldna say 't to a relation, but ye'll maybe no get the offer o't up by, if a' be true."

"What wye, woman?"

"Oh, it's in the wind that the young mistress has set her face again' sperits o' a' sorts, and is no gaun to alloo onything o' the kind ava'. The elders are bonny and angry about it, for it has lang been the custom to brew a stiff gless o' toddy after their business in the manse about Sacrament-time."

Mrs. M'Whinnie pursed up her mouth firmly, and nodded her head twice, as much as to say, "Who ever heard the like o' that?"—then changing the mental point of view **her head** moved several times vertically, which evidently signified that it was not very much worse than she expected. However, **since** she had taken the trouble to **come** so **far she would see for** herself. Under the guidance of the servant **lass** Mrs. M'Whinnie found **her way up to** the manse, **and was** shown **into the drawing-room.** She **had heard** through members **of the family** what a **grand** place the manse was, **but even** her most extravagant dreams of the place **were eclipsed** by the **sight of the** room into which **she had been** ushered. Such droll, and she thought, useless articles of furniture, **she** had never seen in her experience before. What could they all be for, unless for show ? Such cushions and stuffed **seats, it seemed to her,** were beyond **all** reason, as if **a person once down was never expected** to rise again. For herself **she took** the most unyielding chair **she** could **find, and,** lest it should seduce **her** into **too amiable a frame of** mind, she sat sideways on the **one corner of it.** The very pictures on the wall seemed to keep their eyes upon her. They were so life-like, that **she** began to feel ill **at** ease under their scrutiny. They seemed all grand people, from their frilled linen and their **fine** clothes ; and one of **the** female pictures looked **slyly at her** from behind **an** article shaped, as she thought, **like a** peacock's tail, and seemed to enjoy her very uneasiness. **It** was embarrassing sitting thus under **the** view of **her** " betters." What had come over Robin? If he did not meet her at the coach, he had no excuse for delay now that she was under his roof. Here she had sat for at least half an hour (the time was exactly three minutes), and he had not made his appearance. In the midst of these reflections the door opened, and a smart, well-dressed, well-favoured, self-possessed young woman came forward, took the old lady's withered face between her hands, and kissed her.

"Did ever onybody see the like of that!" was the mother-in-law's mental remark. "The bold piece, to kiss a woman she had never seen in her life before! Poor Robin, that had been the way he was taken in!"

"I am so glad to see you," said the young wife, not knowing what was passing through her relative's mind at the moment.

"It's geyan like it," replied Mrs. M'Whinnie, senior, adjusting the ties of her bonnet, that had been disarranged by the unexpected embrace. She would have it out with them now that she had broken ground. "Whaur's Robin?"

"Oh, Mr. M'Whinnie is in his study, but he will join us immediately. Come with me and get off your things, and we'll have such a nice cup of tea presently."

"I hinna mony things to tak' aff—and as for your tea, I'm no heeding for't. It would be a hantle wiser-like if ye would offer me a little sperits after coming aff a lang journey."

It should be said that Mrs. M'Whinnie, senior, was for the moment acting a part which was to some extent inconsistent with her general character and habits, but after what she had heard from Nanse Tannock, she was clear on the necessity of taking this young person down. On the other hand, the young wife, though somewhat disconcerted, resolved not to take the old lady's remarks seriously. She had observed that Scotch people of this class frequently indulged in a kind of grim humour. It was certainly bad manners, and sometimes looked like ill-temper, but it was their way, and they meant no ill by it. It must be true Scotch humour, humour of the subtlest kind, she thought, so subtle, indeed, that the fun of the thing often lay in undiscriminating people taking it seriously. How comical it was of the dear old creature taking the trouble to introduce herself in this charmingly unconventional fashion! This momentary reflection left rather a pleasant expression on her face as she took her mother-in-law by the arm with gentle familiarity, remarking that they would discuss such a lot of matters afterwards, if in the meantime she would "just come to the bedroom and get off her things."

"No ae foot will I move till I get a dram," said the senior Mrs. M'Whinnie, disengaging herself somewhat rudely from the friendly grasp, "since ye have putten me to name it."

"But a cup of warm tea will surely be better for you. Perhaps you do not know that—that I rather disapprove of spirituous liquors."

"My certies!" said the elder lady, drawing herself up to full stature, and looking with close-set lips and drooping eyelids at the slim, lady-like creature before her. "So you disapprove o' sperits? Baith o' ye? Weel, weel, things have come to a bonny pass. Ye'll live on egg-flip, no doubt. But whaur's oor Robin? Puir Robin, ye have long wearied and waited for a grand lady, but, my man, ye've gotten her at last." The old lady flounced past her daughter-in-law, whose appreciation of subtle humour was beginning to decline, and on her way out she met the minister at the door of his study, and the last fling, as she called it, was reserved for him.

"So, so, Robin, this is a fine reception you have arranged for me. We didna think that we were slaving ourselves training ye up for this. But I might have expected it when she sent me that stuff gown. Silk would have been lost on me. You stood calmly by and let your mither be insulted. Weel, I don't wonder at it; for a woman that can prescribe baith meat and drink for the whole parish is no like to be hindered in her on-gauns by a silly coof like you. But I had a silk gown before ever

I saw the face o' either o' ye, and if the Lord spares me to work for it, I'll maybe have anither ane yet before I dee." With this remark she set a steady face towards the door, and went straight out into the gloaming before he had time to say a single word in reply.

Robert M'Whinnie was bewildered; he had just been penning a few sentences of his projected book on "Popular Social Sins." What could he do but follow his irate parent, and, if possible, bring her back and mollify her wounded feelings?

CHAPTER VI.

JAMES THOMSON OF THE GIRTLE.

There was some excitement in Glenbuckie when it became known that the laird of Girtle was dying. He was the tallest, and in some respects the most curt and uncouth man in the parish. When Girtle took a positive dislike to any one, the feeling in his mind was not usually much modified by the lapse of time. William Dickie and he did not get on very well together. He detested William's sanctimonious airs, and William, on his part, deplored his neighbour's loose speech and ungovernable temper. It was said that on a certain occasion Girtle, finding one of William Dickie's sheep drowning in a bog, stalked into the marsh up to the waist, freed the poor creature from the entanglement, and saved its life. William was greatly moved by this act.

"Man, Girtle," he said, the first time they met after this incident, "I 'm glad the Lord put it into your heart to save that sheep o' mine. I didna expect ye would have dune it." Girtle's reply was rough but characteristic.

"Damn ye!" he replied, looking down on his colloquist with inexpressible scorn. "Do ye think because I had cuisten oot wi' you, I had cuisten oot wi' your sheep too?"

Girtle was a bachelor, and was the reputed possessor of considerable means. The only near relative he had was his sister Girzie, who acted as his housekeeper. Girzie and he had frequent brawls, for she had as dour and variable a temper as his own. One of their recent quarrels had not yet been quite squared. It occurred in this manner: He had a monkey and a parrot which were both great favourites of his, and both had been provided for in his will. This was no secret. They were the only creatures in the house, he said, who never contradicted him, and he told Sandy Spiers, his faithful servant man, that if he (Girtle) died he wanted him (Sandy) to take charge of them, and he would find their upkeep no burden, as he had provided for them during the term of their natural life; and, after their decease, Sandy was to succeed them as reversionary legatee. The creatures, however, shortly afterwards, came to an untimely end. Their deaths occurred within such a suspiciously short period of each other, that Girtle, whether rightly or wrongly, suspected his sister Girzie of "putting hand on them." Who else could be interested in getting them out of the way? This was the question he often put to himself. She should not, however, gain by her greed.

His money, most of which he had made himself, by untiring hard work and parsimonious saving, was continually before his eyes. If any one paid especial deference to him, he suspected their motives; while on the other hand, the least show of self-assertion or insubordination on the part of his dependants for whom provision had been made, generally resulted in the making of a new will, or in the insertion of a fresh codicil. For some time he had been in a low condition of health, and was eventually laid down with a malady which the doctor pronounced to be fever.

"Fever!" repeated his sister, as the doctor announced the nature of the trouble. "Losh me, doctor, is it smittle?"

"Ay, it's smittle," replied the doctor. "It is fever of a very malignant type, but I have arranged with Sandy Spiers to take care of your brother, so there is no need of you or the servant-woman running any unnecessary risk."

Girzie went at once to the kitchen to tell Betty M'Clymont, her servant and confidante, the news.

"Eh me!" she said, "if my brother should dee, wouldn't it be gey hard that I daurna see him?"

"It would that, mistress," said Betty, commencing to cry, for she had always a ready supply of tears. "But ye maunna gang into the room, mistress, for they tell me some o' thae fevers are enough to kill a horse, and if ye should baith dee, what would become of me?"

"I ken what I'll do," said Girzie after some cogitation. "I ken what I'll do. I'll put a gless lozen in the door if he turns dangerously ill, and we can tak' turn about in watching. It'll no look so unnatural, and it maunna be said that his ain sister didna watch owre him in his last illness, if it should so happen to be his last."

This expedient, as may be supposed, was not carried out so long as the laird retained consciousness. It was permitted, however, towards the end by the doctor, who was himself somewhat of an eccentric character.

After the fever had nearly run its course, in a brief period of consciousness, James Thomson called Sandy Spiers to his bedside.

"Sandy," he said solemnly, "I'm gaun to dee this time."

"Eh, maister, ye maunna speak that wye," said Sandy.

"It's true, Sandy, and I want to gie ye some directions. D'ye hear?"

"Ay, sir, I hear."

"Weel, listen to what I'm saying. Ye'll find some papers in that writing-table in my room, and here's the key. But mind they're no to be looked at till after the funeral. Are ye listening?"

"Yes, sir, I'm listening, but surely ye'll get better."

"That's no business o' yours; attend to what I'm saying. I have no time to palaver wi' ye. I want a cheap coffin. Mind ye get it big enough, but cheap. Matha Spale will put the brods thegither, and sixpence worth o' black pent will be a' that's needed after that. Then ye'll gang to Troon and get the loan o' Mrs. Lightbody's hearse, twa hours will suffice, and my auld horse 'Broonie' will draw it. Ye'll take her by the head yoursel' and see she gangs cannily and decent-like. Then as to the grave. The lair has never been opened before—and mind it is never opened again, for Girzie maun gang some ither gate. I couldna thole her lying on the tap o' me. Four feet and a half deep will do. Fill in the mools yoursel' and gie the last spadefu' a kindly clap—I'll be watching ye, mind, so tak' care! Are ye hearing me?"

"Ou ay, sir," said Sandy, with a tone of partially suppressed tears in his voice; "I'm hearing ye owre weel."

"What are ye greeting at, ye blockhead? Do ye think I'll be ony waur off whaur I'm gaun? I'm nane o' your professionists that find oot at the hinner end their life has been a' a lee, and are feart to face the truth. I have never made ony great pretence o' saintliness, but I think they'll find oot in the ither worl' that I've aye acted up to what I professed.

If ye have ony tears to spare, greet for the heepocrites, Sandy, but dinna sit there sniftering, as if ye had ony doubts aboot me." The laird, having thus relieved his mind, was forced to pause before resuming his directions as to the post-mortem arrangements. When he was able to do so, Sandy received minute instructions as to who were to be invited to the funeral and as to the reading of the will.

"Is that a' the invitations ye want gi'en?" inquired Sandy, after he had written down the names.

"Is it no plenty? I think ye'll find it'll tak' a guid sup o' whisky to sloken them a'. Wha else would ye have?"

"Weel, sir, I fear ye have forgotten William Dickie."

"No. I haven't forgot William Dickie."

"But his name is no on the list. Ye have kent William Dickie for the last thirty years, and it would look odd-like to leave him oot."

"Weel, I've considered that, but a shauchlie body like him would mak' a sair sicht in a paraud. No, no, Sandy, it canna be. We never have been sic great friends, and the procession will look black enough without William Dickie."

The doctor's opinion, as the days wore on, was that the laird of Girtle could not long survive the severity of the fever, so Girzie and her servant Betty were permitted to take up their position at the glass pane in the door to witness the end.

"Noo, Betty, I'll just lay doon my head and get a wink o' sleep, and ye'll watch, for I am clean worn aff my feet. I'll gie ye the peppermint water—gie a bit swish aboot ye wi't noo and then; but be sure and wauken me if ye see ony change." Their vigils were somewhat protracted, for, as Girzie said, her brother was "geyan teuch." The end, however, came suddenly at last, and it was not long of being noised abroad through the parish that the laird of Girtle was no more.

Sandy Speirs carried out his late master's instructions even to the giving of the "mools" a kindly clap. Such a faithful servant was not likely to fail in performing the last request of a master, who, although somewhat arbitrary, had, on the whole, been very kind to him.

There was only one small hitch about the ceremony. Matha Spale had made the coffin according to instructions, and at the cheapest rate consistent with good workmanship, for, as he said to Speirs—

"It's a' very weel for you, Sandy, to say the laird wanted a cheap thing, wi' no falderals about it, but I maun be able to stand on the heid o' my ain work. I have my name to maintain." But it was found at the "lifting" that Mrs. Lightbody's hearse was too short for the coffin. There was some unseemly work about trying to get it in; at last, however, they secured it with a straw-rope, and Sandy, with the perspiration dropping from his face, took " Broonie " by the head, and the solemn procession moved on.

The funeral over, the most momentous part of the day's proceedings was yet to come—namely, the reading of the will. Everybody was anxious to hear how the laird had left his money.

Girzie's grief was to some extent assuaged, at least for the moment, by the great efforts which she and Betty had to put forth to get a " meat tea " ready for the men coming back from the " yaird."

" They 'll be as hungry as hawks," said Girzie, as she cut up a loaf of bread into half a dozen slices. " I don't know whether ye ever noticed it, Betty, but it 's something really remarkable how folk eat after a burial."

As is customary, there was but a limited and interested number invited to return. There was no lawyer present, for the laird in making his last will —the previous one was full of confusing codicils— had dictated its terms, waited at the lawyer's office till it was extended, paid the charges, and brought it home with him in his pocket, for, as he said, he " wanted no back spangs." The papers were all found as the laird had explained, and after the tea-things had been removed, and Betty had brought a hassock for her mistress's feet, the Rev. Robert M'Whinnie was requested to read the will. With reference to this document, it is only necessary to refer to a couple of clauses.

"To my sister, Girzie, I leave and bequeath the sum of twelve pounds nineteen and sixpence in sterling money, to be paid to her on the fifteenth day of March in each year: this being the sum I had set aside for the maintenance of my late monkey and parrot, and the date of payment being the anniversary of their decease." After making provision for this, and sundry other annuities, the rest of his estate, very much to the amazement of all present, and especially to the principal legatee himself, was bequeathed to Robert Simpson, in grateful remembrance of a "good turn" Robert had once done him, and which he—the testator—declared had not slipped from his memory.

CHAPTER VII.

ROBERT SIMPSON.

As we have already seen, Robert Simpson was a man of humorous mind, but he had also a deliberately kind heart, and when justice had to be done he was not the man to stand aside and let it miscarry. On the morning after the funeral Simpson left Glenbuckie, and was absent for several days. There was much speculation as to the cause of this absence, particularly as it was supposed to have special reference to recent events; consequently the gathering in Nanse Tannock's at the end of the third day was uncommonly large.

"They tell me he gied the minister a call the morning before he left," remarked Matha Spale. "Haplands, you're an elder: did ye hear ocht about it?"

"No much," replied Haplands evasively, not caring to allow that he—a fellow-elder of the Kirk —should be left in absolute ignorance of what had taken place during such an important interview. "No doubt they will want it keepit secret-like, at least for the present time."

"There's no need for ye gieing us a' the oots and ins," said the soutar, willing to compromise.

"No, no," said M'Alpine; "just gie's an inklin' o' what Robert intends doing wi' the siller. They tell me it comes to a bonny penny when a'things are puttin' thegither."

"We maunna tell a' we ken about Robert's intentions," replied Haplands. "But maybe it'll no be ill-pleasing to you to hear that my mistress was doon at the Girtle."

"Ay, noo, there's something—let's hear the news. Girzie's temper'll be no ae bit sweeter for the turn things have ta'en."

"No ae bit," said Haplands, encouraged by this appropriate way of putting the matter. "Ye ken Girzie and oor mistress never got on very weel wi' ane anither." No one wondered much at that, for it was well enough known that the speaker's wife had a "sorry tongue." "But ye see, we thocht we'd just let bygones be bygones, in the face o' trouble."

"A Christian-like thing!" Matha Spale interposed. "Weel?"

"We was curious too, ye ken, just to hear hoo the harrows were gaun, noo that Robert Simpson had been left the rough o' the siller."

"Natural, natural," continued the cartwright encouragingly.

"Weel, ye see, what will the woman do but just

fa' on oor ane like a wulcat, regairdin' some stories she should have tell't Janet Pyat a guid whilie sin'."

"There, noo," deplored M'Alpine, "and I suppose the mistress got no sense oot o' her ava."

"No that muckle, for it was just Janet Pyat could say this, and Janet Pyat could say that, till oor ane just tell't her she shouldna craw so crouse, for twelve pounds nineteen and sixpence o' sterling money o' a yearly tocher wouldna gang so far that she could afford to affront folks that were disposed to be friendly wi' her."

"And what said she to that, noo? That was intil her."

"Oh, she says, 'Ye can just gang hame, and tell Janet Pyat and ony ither o' your confederates, that they're no to fash their heads about me, for if that's what you have come to ferrit out, I may tell ye I have ample provision made for me, although I should live to be as auld as Methusalum, or in ither words, till I am nearly as auld as yoursel'.'"

"Weel, that was a guid ane," cried M'Alpine, striking his thigh with thoughtless approbation.

"It was geyan impident," remarked several members of the company sympathetically.

"I mean it was geyan impident," said the farmer, checking his levity, and swaying to the popular side with customary consistency. "It was just geyan impident to speak that wye to a woman who had called to make peace wi' her."

"And that was all your mistress got, I suppose," remarked Matha Spale.

"'Deed it was enough. I have seldom seen her in sic a rage. She was sair putten aboot."

"What do ye think she meant by saying 'provision was made for her'?" inquired the cartwright. "She would be splorin' a bit, no doubt."

"Very likely, for she canna have that muckle saved o' her ain."

"I'll no say but she's ettling to dispute the will," said the soutar.

"Gore! and didna that cross my mind too!" M'Alpine remarked. "It's a very likely thing."

"But nobody could say that Girtle was oot o' his mind when the will was made," said Matha Spale. "That is the only ground that a will can be broke on, as I understand it."

"But does it no seem an onjust thing too," remarked M'Clymont after deep consideration; "just to think o' him leaving the feck o' his siller to a stranger when he had ane o' his ain flesh and bluid to inherit it? Dod, I think there should be some law again' that!" This was an abstract remark, and meant to apply to the human family generally, for it may have been observed that Girzie Thomson, from whatever cause, was held in no especial esteem by those present.

Jamie Pinkie, who up to this time sat in a corner nursing a dignified reticence, now spoke out.

"I canna allow that remark to pass onchallenged, M'Clymont. What for should the wealth o' the country gang spinning round in a circle o' useless aristocrats—no that Girzie Thomson is an aristocrate, but it's the same principle—leaving a'body ootside o't in poverty, wi' hardly a lair o' earth to bury themsel's in. That's the wye o't, according to the present laws. You and me have been born outside o' that charmed circle, and, what's mair, the law has barred the door again' us ever winnin' in. Ye ken my views on thae twa curses o' the country —entail and primogeniture. No reform bill will ever be perfect that doesna abolish them; and yet you, M'Clymont, a puir blanket-weaver, wi' nothing but a set o' heddles between you and eternity, will sit there and talk about the makin' o' laws to do owre again what is even now keeping us sitting here i' the dirt. Man, ye dinna ken what you're sayin'!"

M'Clymont began to perceive hazily that there were consequences involved in his words which he had not dreamed of, but even with the aid of the tailor's attempted elucidation, he could not see that his reasoning applied to the special case under consideration. So he dared to remark, "But surely, Jamie, bluid is thicker than water!"

"Bluid!" cried the tailor with scornful emphasis, ignoring the point at issue; "bluid was a' o' ae thickness when the Almichty first opened the Yaird o' Eden to us. Your bluid and mine is maybe no so thick as it should be; but what is the cause o' that? I tell ye it's the laws o' the country. Is it right that ae man should have thousands o' acres to colour and thicken his bluid on, while you and me should dwine awa' in a room and kitchen, and draw our sustenance frae a dozen square feet o' a kail-yaird?" The tailor was now fairly roused to rough but eloquent speech. He had the political ball with all its defects and one-sided enactments at his feet, and he was nothing loath to kick it.

While the discussion was proceeding the mail-coach from Ayr had dropped Robert Simpson at the cross-roads' outside of the village, and the first person he encountered was William Dickie. William was there apparently by pure accident, and said he was only taking a bit dander over to Nanse Tannock's to hear the news. After the usual greeting, the two elders walked on for some moments in silence.

"Man, Robert, the ways o' the Lord are geyan strange." This remark was accompanied by a sigh that was meant to be solemnly impressive. "'In the morning we are like grass which groweth up. In the morning it flourisheth and groweth up, in the evening it is cut down and withereth.' It is a true word that says, 'we spend our years like a tale that is told.'"

"This is good," thought Simpson, "but the body might speer at once what I intend doing with puir Girtle's siller without sic a sanctimonious leading up to it." "Yes, William, geyan like what we read o' in story-books," was the expressed reply.

"The seed o' the wicked shall be cut off," continued William. "Isn't it very remarkable? Here is a woman—little better nor himsel', if a' be true—left a lone creature i' the world, wi' hardly as much in her hand as will keep saul and body thegither. Yet he had plenty, I am tauld."

"Ou ay, plenty," said Simpson. "Girtle was a rare hand for saving siller."

"Noo, ye see that, but he couldna take it wi' him, Robert; nane o' us can do that. As Dr. Plunket used to say, 'there are no pockets i' the shroud.' I'm supposing there'll be three, or maybe four thousand, when a's dune."

"I wouldna be surprised," remarked Robert dryly.

"Eh, but that's a large sum na." William paused to ruminate. "It's a great responsibility, this siller, when folk look at it in a richt wye. I was kin' o' cheered, though, when I heard the stewardship o't had been intrusted to you."

Simpson suspected what was coming, and replied encouragingly—

"So you would. Did ye think I would mak' a guid steward, William?"

"It's a serious duty," admitted William; "but the Lord seldom sends responsibilities on his ain folk without giving grace to bear them. It's wonderfu'," he continued, with another sigh (this time, of Christian resignation), "it's truly wonderfu'. He sends ane back and anither forat, but we maunna complain when it's His ain hand that does it. Here am I, wi' a' my last year's cheese lying in the laft sweating themselves awa' to mere skeletons, waiting for a turn o' the market; and they tell me they're back twa shillings the day."

"They are that," said Robert; "the market was geyan backward. But ye were owre greedy, William. I advised ye to sell last year when the prices were ordinar' good."

"Weel, it's a gey spite I didna take your advice. It would have been telling me a ten-pound note. Then there was that beast that died i' the spring."

"I have told ye before I didna pity ye much in that," said Simpson. "A man that winna lift his beast out o' a sheuch on the Sabbath-day deserves to lose it."

"But we maun reverence the Word," said William. "Things may gang wrang, but we should aye haud on by it. Is it no written, 'Whosoever doeth any work on the Sabbath, that soul shall be cut off from among his people'? I didna forget the law o' mercy, as ye ken, for I put an ordinar stout plank under the beast's head, and left a pickle gress beside it; surely the bruit micht 'a tholed till Monday! But the Lord gies, and the Lord takes away."

"The Lord has to stand the blame o' a guid deal," thought Robert.

"Weel, in the circumstances," continued William blandly, "I thocht ye maybe wouldna press me for that fifty pound ye lent me last Candlemas was a twelvemonth—at least no till things take a turn."

"As to that," said Robert, "I wouldna like to make ony rash promise. Ye ken it should have been paid at Martinmas. It's a token o' guid stewardship to look weel after the siller."

"But, between elders," remonstrated William.

"Weel, between elders, it should be different so far, that they ought to be fully as particular as ither folk in being honest wi' ane anither. But here's Mrs. Tannock's, and, on my word, if that creature Jamie Pinkie's no trying to maltreat that decent sailor body, William IV. Od! William! we maun e'en gang ben and save the king."

The company rose to greet Robert as he entered. "Keep your seats," he said. "I was only passing with William Dickie, when I heard the tailor there —pointing to Jamie Pinkie—dashing himsel' to pieces against the mailed body o' the king, and as I kent it was gey dry, no to say profitless work, I thought I would come ben and offer ye a dram. Nanse, bring in the tappit hen."

It is needless to say that this remark was received with demonstrative applause. "Send it round,' said Robert, as Nanse placed the sonsie measure on

F

the table. "I have just come off the coach, after a cauld drive, and though I have barely got the command o' my tongue, I feel it is expected that I should propose a toast. Doubtless, ye have heard the sentiment before, but it's a guid ane, I can tell ye." He glanced round the apartment, with lips firmly set, and chin well in the air, pausing the while to emphasise the undelivered sentiment.

"Now sirs," he said, "may—the hinges of friendship *never* rust!" The toast was pledged with deep and thirsty enthusiasm.

"Well," continued Simpson, "having saved the king, and oiled the hinges o' friendship, it is maybe time to go, for the man who prefers the smoky air o' a change-house to his ain cosy fire-end, especially after being so long away from it as I have been, shouldna have a home. But as I have become an heir since we last met, and seeing the event was as unexpected as it was undeserved, maybe I should tell ye what I propose doing wi' Girtle's siller."

"Men," said the soutar, rising in his place with a respectful and dignified air, "we a' ken brawly, that whatever Robert Simpson does or has dune wi' Girtle's siller is richt, and we'll no be sorry to hear o't frae his ain lips if he cares to tell us; but before he proceeds to that part o' the story, I'm sure we would a' like to hear o' the 'guid turn' that was dune to the laird, but which Robert Simpson, in his modesty, may wish to conceal. We a' ken his knack o' doing guid turns by stealth, but Girtle wasna in the habit o' taking a liking to onybody without guid cause."

"There is no accounting for some things," said the legatee, pausing, and looking around the company as if he were about to take them frankly into his confidence, "but my firm belief is that the Dadians were at the bottom o't. You may talk about the Crackanalians and the Nickadumphians as ye like, for I don't like either o' them, as ye ken; but after a careful, and I may say lifelong, study o' the whole tribe, I am convinced that the thing was entirely due to the state o' the Dadians at the time. Girtle was a guid soul, and the joke was fine enough while it lasted, though maybe it was just carried owre far. I have, however, squared it now, for, in these papers you see in my hand, I have re-established the true succession to the laird's fortune, and made owre the whole box and dice o't to his sister Girzie, for, whatever Jamie Pinkie may say to the contrary, it justly and legally belongs to her as the next o' kin."

CHAPTER VIII.

THE MINISTER'S RECORD (*continued*).

Two important events have occurred since I indited my last record. These I might truthfully divide into three heads, for, while the first refers to the passing of the Reform Bill, the second leads me to realise the solemn fact that the Lord has placed on my unworthy shoulders the momentous responsibility of twin children. As to the Reform Bill, God only knows whether it is a good and safe measure for the country. With all this outcry going on against patronage, one is naturally constrained to inquire whether the Church is not also in danger, especially in the hands of a newly enfranchised, wilful, comparatively ignorant people. My wife's first cousin, who is a curate in Manchester, sent me a most kind letter of congratulation on the double blessing that had fallen to my own lot in the birth of twin bairns; but his joy regarding that event was small compared with the ecstasy experienced by him over the success of the Liberal party in carrying their great measure of Reform.

Well, after all, looked at from his point of view, perhaps this is not strange. The English Church does not allow its members to take much part in the management of ecclesiastical concerns, so that he can only see this important question from its political side. With us it is different: the common people have hitherto, it is true, been debarred from taking any active share in matters of political import, but the Church has always been open to them, and in recent movements they have not been slow to exercise their masterfulness. One success leads on to another—what then is more likely than that they may turn their newly-acquired political power, especially at the present moment of agitation, into an instrument to effect dangerous mutations in the constitution of the Church itself? With this on my mind, it is natural that the political items in my good cousin's letter should have been received with less sympathy than those which referred to my own immediate and undoubted personal blessings. I have not told my wife a word about these apprehensions, for although she has had a wonderful recovery, she is not yet by any means strong. These national and family agitations have a marvellous influence over the mind in incapacitating it for literary or studious work. It is three long months now since I added a line to my work on "Popular Social Sins;" indeed, it has been with difficulty that I have been able to prepare for my ordinary pulpit ministrations, for the accession to my family overtook us with much greater celerity than my wife and I reckoned upon; and to add to our discomfiture, there was no one in the household who had any skill in the management of infant bairns. Janet Pyat, whose evangelical tendencies have of late been growing more pronounced, had some words with my wife on the place and power of the civil magistrates in ecclesiastical matters. The upshot was that Janet left the house. This, as may be jaloused, was a great grief to me, for she was not only an old and trusty servant with whom it was hard to part, but in view of what I knew was soon likely to happen, her leaving was doubly vexatious. However, when the event did take place, the Lord was very kind to us, for He enlarged her heart in so much that she at once came back to us in a spirit of great magnanimity. It is truly a fine, or I might say, a poetical sensation to feel these two helpless and innocent cherubs nestling with instinctive trustfulness in one's bosom. The Psalmist's words have of late been borne in on my mind with singular meaning and power, for we are in truth "fearfully and wonderfully made." For my own part, I never hitherto cared much for infant bairns, and I often wondered how grown-up people, especially men, could take unfeigned pleasure in them, but that feeling has undergone a mysterious change. The great and all-wise Creator seems to have unsealed a dormant well-spring in my heart —it must, I suppose, have been there before— for I can now not only tolerate, but in point of fact, I never tire of gazing at them. They have such marvellously queer ways, and make such queer faces; while they beat the air with their helpless cluster of clenched fingers that you would think they were fighting for dear life with dangerous, but invisible foes. There seems also to be a most sympathetic and tender connection between them, for when one begins to cry, the other purses its lips with sweet sensitiveness, and immediately there is a chorus, or as one might say with stricter accuracy, a duet of a most plaintive and touching character. Truly the study of children is an elevating and refining thing. Even Janet Pyat seems less severe, as she sits between the cradles performing little duties pertaining to the requirements of infancy, and touching the "rockers" with her foot when any evidence of restlessness occurs. Such a turn-up as our new arrivals have made in our house! Our grand withdrawing-room has been transformed into a nursery, and indeed that gives me but moderate concern, for we really made little use of it, and it is to my mind more pleasing to know that it is occupied by one's own family, than that it should be kept for the reception of people who either go away and grumble at our extravagance, or turn up their noses and say that it can bear but poor comparison with their own.

Janet Pyat, the other day, did a most humorsome and canty thing, at the which my wife laughed in a most hearty, not to say dangerous manner, considering the bairns were little better than three weeks old. What should she do but dress the infants in their long gowns and dainty white "mutches," decked with pink ribbon! That done, she placed them in the paternal arms, skipped off to the kitchen with the agility of a young person and brought up the servant lassie, while there I stood a show to be laughed at by my own wife and my two lawfully hired serving-women. I felt inclined to rebuke Mrs. Pyat for this liberty, but as I suspected my wife was at the bottom of the ploy, and as it provoked so much hearty and withal innocent merriment, I could not find in my heart to do it.

It is quite true, as my ruling elder William Dickie so frequently says, that the ways of Providence are strange. When I brought home my dear wife to Glenbuckie, she was very hopeful of working great reforms amongst the people. She was, it must be admitted, without much knowledge of the national character, having been brought up in fine English schools, nor had she during her sojourn in the North fully apprehended how conservative the Scottish people are of established forms and customs.

Her views as to adopting the standing attitude in church during divine praise were so bitterly opposed when I mooted the matter privately to my session, that to save schism, or I should say the disruption which might have ensued, I felt constrained to act with prudence, and abandon the proposed innovation, at least for the time, as hopeless. I was, moreover, admonished by the rupture which had taken place in the neighbouring parish of Kilmaurs, as to the danger of interfering with established forms of worship. The question was indeed a subtle one, and had reference to the point of time at which the officiating minister should handle the elements at the Communion. This led to great diversity of opinion and warmth of argument, one party declaring the bread should be lifted by the minister before the giving of thanks, and the other that it should not be handled till he was about to distribute it to the communicants. The controversy waxed so exceeding hot that there was a grievous split in the congregation, which led to the establishment of two distinct bodies—the one being known as the "Lifters," and the other as the "Antilifters." This scandal had occurred, to be sure, amongst the body of seceders known as Antiburghers, and was outwith the Established Church. But though the breach had since been healed, it behoved me in such kittle times to be on my guard against allowing a rock of offence, or, in more appropriate terms, a stumbling-block to be placed in the way of my simple but well-meaning people. My wife's views on the temperance question being so entirely new in these parts, were also looked upon with disfavour, and considered to be dangerous innovations. It was for a time painful to see ideas, good in themselves, and, on the whole, so well intentioned, set down to the influence of strange doctrines learned in foreign and heretical schools. Indeed, I was myself disposed to put a gentle check upon this well-meant zeal, seeing, as I did, that it might lead to open hostility, when suddenly—let me say it reverently — a good Providence came upon the scene, and filled her hands with the care of twin children. Nothing could have been more opportune, or I might say, timely. It was a serious thing to think of the Sacrament coming on, with its various meetings at the manse, and with the possible, nay, I might almost say certain, expression of my wife's dissent against the toddy after Monday's dinner, which, I am sure, would have aroused hostile feelings in the minds of the session. But with a little time for reflection, as she is now bound to take, I am persuaded she will have the wisdom to let well-enough alone.

Poor Maggie Winlestrae, misguided creature, has had a sore trial. Maggie's misfortune, in spite of the asseverations of the mistress of Haplands, was passed over as lightly as the laws of the Church would allow, for really, though she is a glaiket and unstable being, she submitted to the chastisement due to her offence with exemplary readiness. But while she was ready, poor thing, to bear the blame, all we could do would not induce her to disclose the name of the partner in her sin. Though we jaloused who he was, in the absence of direct proof, the session was powerless to lay the charge at his door. By the tragic occurrence which has just occurred, I opine we can trace the hand of an avenging Judge pouring the vials of His just wrath upon the cruel and designing man who stole away poor Maggie's peace of mind. Though the evidence is wonderfully circumstantial, it would be unbecoming of me to mention his name in this record. The lad, however, was far above her station, but he was a youth of a light, or I might say frivolous, mind—being no less than the son of a colliery proprietor, at present residing near the seashore for the health of his family. He was college-bred, which makes the case even worse—for what is the use of education unless it teaches us to hold a firm hand upon our sinful lusts and passions, and trains us to set a pattern of virtue and godliness to the depraved and ignorant around us? Indeed, I have pondered so deeply on this case that, in the good providence of God, I have been led to make special note of it to be embraced in my book on "Popular Social Sins." Though, as I have said, we could not trace this great transgression of Bible-law to the lad's door, William Dickie, who has such unerring judgment, or I might say instinct, in such matters, entertained the gravest suspicions regarding him. I have no doubt, however, but he was led on by Maggie's engaging manners, and by her desire to wed a lad that was above her in station. But, alas! it has come to a sore end. After Maggie's admonishment by the session, it was bruited abroad that her admirer had been ordered by his parents to take a sea-voyage. It was said to be for his health, but I believe the distemper was more a moral than a physical one. The vessel set sail from Ardrossan harbour. She was as fine a ship as you could clap eyes on, and was under command of William Plunket, the eldest son of the former minister of Glenbuckie, a steady, God-fearing man. But the hand of the Lord was upon her—contrar winds prevailed, followed by a storm of rain and wind, the like of which we have not known in the parish for many a day. Chimney-stalks were blown down; the roof was clean stripped off William Dickie's byre; and the manse itself, to the serious detriment, and I may say alarm, of Mrs. M'Whinnie, who was at the time in a very critical condition of health, was denuded of at least a full bushel-basket of slates. But what was worse than all, the noble vessel, which the day before had steered out of port in such hope and pride, was blown back on the

Horse Island, and at break of day poor Maggie Winlestrae was found sitting on the shore, wet through with sea-spray and rain, with the head of the lad who had been the source of all her misery on her lap. It was a most melancholy sight, and very touching, to see the self-forgetfulness of the lassie after all she had tholed. He had been washed ashore from the raft on which he had vainly tried to save himself, and, saddest of all, it was found that the poor infant she carried with her was lying dead at her breast. It was enough to break the hardest heart to think of all this self-devotion and suffering. No wonder the tears fill my eyes as I write, for one cannot forget how hard it would be to lose the dear little bairnies that have nestled in one's bosom, and which, at the present moment, are lying so snugly in the withdrawing-room above me, in their downie cots, under the stern but vigilant eye of their watchful nurse, Janet Pyat.

PART THIRD

CHAPTER IX.

TAMMAS SCOUGALL, THE MOLECATCHER.

THE first swallow had been observed for some days twittering about the amber pools of Crosbie burn, and Willie Tweeddale, the shepherd, remarked the circumstance with inward satisfaction, for the lambing season had just closed, leaving a fair brood of lambs, and now this small grey weather prophet spoke hopefully, by its presence, of balmy night-winds, and soft green nibblings on the hillsides for the tender flock.

It was but the first week of May, yet the hedges had burst into leaf, and little branches of hawthorn blossom might be seen in knotted clusters amongst the green mist of foliage that was everywhere visible in the neighbourhood of Crosbie glen. The snowdrop had passed away early under the genial warmth of the sun, the crocus and primrose had followed in natural succession, the latter might be seen in luminous clusters on mossy banks, and under the soft fronds of delicately expanding ferns. The lark had been in the sky for hours, thrilling the air with gentle pulsations of song, before Tammas Scougall opened his door and stepped out into the dewy freshness of the summer morning. The sun had climbed above the Baidlands, and the long waves were glittering in his rosy beams as they shouldered each other gently towards the shore. Yonder stood the stately Goatfell in the virgin light, without a shred of vapour to drape the porphyry shoulders. Bute lay in slumberous shade; and beyond, over pale-green stretches of sea, a lighthouse caught the eye of the sun, and shone out in conspicuous whiteness. Tammas Scougall slung on his burden of wire traps—the badges of his profession—and passed through an opening in the hedge, opposite his own door, into a neighbouring field, where the long swing of his heavy boots, as he brushed aside the shining dew, left a dark green track behind him in the grass. On the other side of the field a footpath led up past a wood to a small bridge in the glen, immediately above the waterfall. Though Tammas was fully a quarter of a mile from this point, he could hear the fresh cool water first hissing, and then plunging into the deep rocky caldron, where graceful hart's-tongue ferns, tender lichens, and other plants of nameless grace and beauty, flourished in the refreshing mist that hung about the seething pool. As he passed along, rabbits ran helter-skelter from the green fields, through mysterious interstices in the rude stone dyke, and disappeared in the wood.

Then a swift-footed hare, that had lingered unduly over its feast of young wheat in one of William Dickie's fields, turned up the white tip of an excited tail, and made off towards the long bent covers on the sandy uplands.

The molecatcher was but a poor hand at speech, though he had a habit of thinking, and on some rather dangerous questions dared to hold opinions of his own. On the whole, he was an honest, a sober, God-fearing man, who might have cherished hopes of one day becoming a member of the Glenbuckie kirk-session, had it not been bruited abroad that he was rather shaky in his mind as to the existence of a physical hell.

"Sperits canna burn," he had said the night before to the dyker, as they stood at the style before parting for the night. "There's nae substance i' them, man. I suppose ye'll no deny that angels are sperits, and ye'll mind what Dr. Plunket, wha was a deep thinker in speritual things, used to say aboot angels, 'A sword canna pierce them,' he said, 'and as for yer cannon-balls, well, they wud just wap through them, and no do them wan bit o' hairm.'"

"I ken nothing aboot angels," replied the dyker bluntly, but honestly feeling that his friend was fighting wide of the point between them, "but this I ken, we are tauld i' the Word 'it is sown a natural body, it is raised a speritual body.' Noo, ye see, there is the body, and so lang as there is a body, ye needna threep on me that there's nae fire and nae burning. Man, Tammas, I would like to believe that what ye say is richt, for sca'din 's no a canny thing; but dae awa' wi' the fire, and what's to become o' us? Ministers micht shut the kirk doors, and tak' to trades like oursel's, for what would be the sense o' listening to lang sermons, payin' teens, and a' the rest? No, no, Tammas, I would earnestly advise ye to tak' care that it's no putten into yer head by the Foul Thief himsel', for it's far owre comfortable a belief to be true."

This was a new and painful view of the matter, which the molecatcher could neither establish nor refute. While he stepped up the glen in the fresh morning light, he was turning this and other kindred matters over in his mind; but it required a continuous spell of meditation in this congenial field before he could settle down and single out any given point to grapple with. He had crossed the bridge, and was passing noiselessly along the narrow, mossy loaning, with its close undergrowth of furze on either side, and its upper growth of spruce and larch, whose fresh green tassels almost formed an archway over his head, while the shadows cast by the graceful young shoots waved softly at his feet like daffodils. Suddenly, the inward commotion was forgotten by the call of an outward sense. He paused to listen, with an upward look, and with his ear set to the wind. He laid down his traps, and went forward cautiously for a few steps, clearing the bushes aside gently with his hands, and listening as he went. The sound he had heard was like the mewing of a wounded hare. The narrow pathway now opened to a roomier space, into one corner of which the sun peeped. Here it shone upon something which made the simple molecatcher stand aghast—for in that particular spot lay an infant, wrapped in a thick grey, home-made shawl, with a little pink wry face, which gave unmistakable evidence of annoyance at being so indelicately stared at by the sun. Tammas took off his bonnet, and blessed himself. He stood stock-still, with a superstitious fear stirring about his heart, and " prinkling " at the roots of his hair. Was it a fairy, a brownie, or a witch-wean? Fairies, he knew, were represented as little creatures dressed in green. His mother had once seen a large family of them on a moonlight night in an orchard near the big house in which she served, but they vanished when they saw her. This little person was not dressed in green, and it certainly showed no signs of vanishing. He had never heard of brownies or fairies appearing in open day. Its general appearance was almost sufficient to lead him to suppose it was a witchwean, as it lay there with its wee thrawn face blinking uncomfortably at the obtrusive light. Tammas had no skill of children, for though his wife, Jean, and he had been married for twelve years at the previous Candlemas, they had no family. He had contemplated this object at a safe distance so long without anything happening that he concluded there was no immediate danger, so he took a few steps gently forward, still holding his bonnet reverently in his hand. When he came near, he put his hands on his knees, and let himself down cautiously till his own face descended to within a couple of feet or so of the child's. This posture now cut off the sun's rays, and the tiny face gradually settled into a more pleasing expression. It did not seem the least afraid of him. If this was a spirit, it was a happy and familiar one, for when he touched the little pink, transparent cheek with the point of one of his rough fingers, the small toothless mouth stretched horizontally into a pleasant grin. He touched it again, first on one cheek and then on the other, to make perfectly sure that it was a creature of flesh and blood, and at each touch the small mouth widened, and the little cheeks dimpled so prettily, that he knelt down and raised it in his strong uncouth hands, and felt pleased to think that, if this little miracle of life had wings, they were tightly folded under the close wrappages of a substantial home-made shawl, and could not, for the present at least, carry it away. Slowly it dawned upon his mind that the nurse or guardian of the child might be near by, so he held it close to his breast with one hand, and guarded it from the branches with the other, while he went a few steps further along the path. There was a slight rustling in the thicket ahead of him, but the rabbits were running so thickly under the cover that he concluded that the disturbance must have been caused by them. He called out several times, but no answer came, so he resolved to take the small foundling home, and consult his wife, Jean, as to what was to be done with it.

As may be imagined, when the matter was reported to the kirk-session, which at that period had the duty and privilege of administering the Poor-Law, it caused no little stir throughout the parish. The session held three several meetings, but their investigations failed to find any clew to the parentage of the child. This could hardly be considered strange, as the parishes had no system of reciprocal action, and each was so much bound up in its own affairs, that any person so inclined might steal out of the one parish into the other, and leave a similar burden on it, without fear of being detected. Naturally, there was much interesting speculation amongst the gossips on the unusual discovery.

"Do you really think that Molie kens naething aboot that wean?" inquired Mrs. Haplands, with a subtle look, as she and Mrs. Dickie walked up the brae next Sunday from the kirk.

"Weel, woman," said the other, "didna that cross my mind, too? How strange that we should baith think o't!"

"Molie has never been considered soun' i' the doctrines, ye ken; and they tell me he says there's nae deevil ava."

"Isn't it awfu' just to think o' there being nae deevil, Mrs. Dickie? When a man wins the length o' sayin' there's nae deevil, he canna be trustit verra far. But we maun gang doon the morn, pretending to see the wean, ye ken, and we'll find oot whether his ain wife believes the story."

Arrangements were made accordingly that they should carry out this purpose next day. The result may be gathered from their conversation on the way home.

"Onything liker Tammas Scougall in flesh and bluid I never saw," said Mrs. Haplands with stern emphasis, when they had got safely round the gable of the molecatcher's house.

"Eh! Isna't vexing that we canna get to the bottom o't? Puir woman, she believes the whole story; and didna ye see how she flang up her fit at me when I speert if she was perfect sure she didna jalouse who its faither was?"

"Mrs. Dickie," said her interlocutor with grim decision, "we maunna alloo the session to pay a penny for the upkeep o' the wean; it would be a premium on sin. That fa's to be settled at next meeting, ye ken. I'll warrant ye my man will vote again ony sic allowance."

Meantime, the undemonstrative hearts of the

worthy couple in the **glen were** beginning **to** soften into genial tenderness **over** this fresh rosebud **of life,** which fate had so unexpectedly thrown upon their path. **It drew them together in one common interest**—it **was** the golden link between heart and heart, which life **to** them hitherto had **lacked.** Before the subject **of** maintenance fell to **be discussed by the** session, **the** molecatcher and his wife had **made up** their minds **that they would not** accept **any** aliment in support of the child. Certain members **of** the session had determined that, if the foundling was **to** be supported by parochial **funds,** some other person than the molecatcher's wife would have to **be** found to **nurse it.** The intimation of their decision, however, prevented **the** discussion of a subject which would have been **keenly, and, in all** likelihood, acrimoniously debated, **for public opinion on** this matter **was** divided; but those **who** entertained suspicions **felt** that **they were now** supported **by** fresh evidence, **so** that **the** scandal received new **and** freer circulation. Fortunately, the molecatcher **and** his wife were too much enamoured of their charge, and **too** anxious for its welfare, to **know what was going** on about them. Mrs. Scougall had gone deep into drawers and presses, and had turned out certain infinitesimal items of dress that had been prepared in sly corners, **and at odd** moments, over twelve years ago—in **anticipation of** hopes that had never been realised. These **she** brought forward now without a blush, and sat down with scissors and needle to adapt them to present requirements. Robert Simpson had sent them a cradle; and Whinnyriggs promised to supply them with fresh milk from a special cow as long as they required it; so, looking at the matter all round, they felt that they were in many ways gainers by the transaction.

On these long evenings of early summer, the molecatcher was as happy in his observant idleness as his wife was in her cutting and sewing. The whole thing was a pleasant mystery to him. When his duties for the day were over, he would seldom move beyond the door, unless it might be to snatch a hurried smoke, for he would not smoke indoors now. During these happy evenings he would sit for hours in contemplative silence, with a dream-like smile on his face, like the fading memory of some happy experience, watching and studying the solicitude which, late in life, had suddenly sprung up in the household: now lending a hand to hold the little wooden cog while the tiny creature was being fed; now touching the cradle when a restless head, stirred by a passing dream, moved on the downy pillow; or now shaking with tender emotion, while his wife, with a half humorous and half serious smile at his awkwardness, would lay the fragile handful of life in his great arms, with the pleading admonition, "Noo, dinna be coorse wi't." These were very pleasant evenings in the molecatcher's humble bothie, and these were the experiences and emotions which made the honest couple feel that the balance of profit lay on their own side.

When the first few days of work and anxiety had passed away, an important question began to grow on the matronly mind, until at last she had to speak to her husband. This question was the christening of the bairn. It was, at best, "a frail slip o' a creatur', and what if it should be ta'en awa' before it was kirstened?" This was too dreadful a hazard to be contemplated calmly; but the feeling became more intense day by day as she found out in spite of all her care that the bairn was not thriving. Tammas' wider views prevented him seeing this matter in the same strong light; still there was a remnant of the old superstition in his mind which led him, at least, to respect his wife's fears, and, ultimately, to yield to her solicitations. The session had numerous meetings over this perplexing request. The child was, in the best view of the matter, sprung of questionable parentage. The father and mother ought to be "dealt with" in accordance with the rules of the Church; but when there was no father and no mother, who was to become responsible for the vows which the ordinance imposed? This difficulty having been met by the molecatcher volunteering to accept this responsibility, it was felt the case was advanced a stage, but then the sponsor's fitness to discharge such a duty had to be considered.

This investigation was remitted to William Dickie and the minister, with instructions that they were to report thereon to a future meeting.

While these discussions were proceeding, Mrs. Scougall was in a very unhappy frame of mind. Her little charge had taken a "brash" of a serious nature, so serious, indeed, that Dr. Gebbie had to be called in. Though Tammas was anxious to satisfy his wife's desires with regard to baptism, he had been soured and annoyed by the spirit that had characterised the proceedings up to this point, and by the mean insinuations which, in a casual way, had reached his ears, so that, when at last he was summoned to the manse to meet his "betters," he was not in a very amiable frame of mind. The minister was inclined, for the sake of peace, to be lenient; but the coarse, blunt questions and insinuations of the elder provoked this simple-minded man beyond the point of decorous prudence.

"Ye ask me if I believe in a hell," he replied to one of William Dickie's leading questions, with a flash of fire in his eye.

"Weel, I didna believe in the hell that ye believe in before I cam' here, but it's plain to me if ever ye get to heaven, there is so muckle dross in ye, that ye'll need a real fire to burn it oot."

We may believe the only thing that hindered the elder from rending his garments at this remark was the thought that they would either have to be replaced or repaired. The minister, however, interposed, and said that the rite of baptism would have to be postponed. Tammas went away with a heavy heart, and with words almost amounting to profanity on his tongue.

"Weel?" inquired his wife anxiously, as he came home with a flushed face.

"It's no use," he replied hopelessly, "they have set their face again' it."

His wife laid down her head on the little form on her knees, and cried aloud.

"The wean's deein'," she sobbed, "the wean's deein', and what are we to do? Oh, Tammas, can ye no do 't yersel'?" What could he do? He was stirred to the very heart by his wife's entreaty and tears. After all these days and nights of weary anxiety, he would do anything to give her comfort and peace.

"Yes," he said solemnly, "I can do it if ye want me. After a', it matters but little wha does it, so be 's it 's dune in humble reverent faith. Jean, if it 'll gie ye peace, I 'll kirsten the wean."

He went and brought a cup of cold water, and sat down on a stool at her feet. It was a trying moment, but his whole soul was stirred by the urgency of the case. For some minutes he bent his head reverently in silent supplication, then he spoke out with a voice full of emotion, "Lord, Thoo kens we are puir creatures, and kenna weel what to do.

Oh, take this wee dearie into Thy heavenly kingdom. In Thoo's ain name, we noo kirsten her Jean Greenwood. We have ettled richt; but, O Lord, gie us forgiveness if we have dune wrang!"

The crystal drops of water, that fell from the brown horny fingers on the small placid brow, were mingled with passionate drops of affection that were less cold. Mrs. Scougall looked up with shining eyes. The final struggle on the little face was but dimly seen through the tearful mist, but there was joy as well as sorrow in her heart, for the little pilgrim, whose journey had been so short, had not passed into the ranks of the Church Triumphant without its name.

* * * * *

About a week after the little foundling was laid in the parish churchyard, the post carrier delivered an anonymous letter addressed to Tammas Scougall, which gave his wife and himself not a little surprise. The packet, which bore the Kilmarnock postmark, contained a couple of one-pound bank-notes, accompanied by a letter indifferently written and spelled.

This letter told with pathetic simplicity the old story of a woman loving above her station, of unwise confidence, and of subsequent desertion. After her child was born, she was helpless and friendless. She confessed with shame the sin of having thrown her own burden upon others, but she did not desert the child with the intention of causing its death.

She had stood concealed till it was safely borne off in strong arms to a home more comfortable than she could hope to provide for it. She had expected one day to be able to make herself known and repay them for all their trouble; but she had just heard of the child's death, and now in deep grief had sent them her first earnings as some small acknowledgment of their kindness. The letter concluded abruptly, and was here and there blurred and blotted with tears.

Tammas afterwards carried the communication to Robert Simpson, and desired him to make what use of it he might think proper, in order to silence the cruel slanders which the bairn's brief sojourn under his roof had raised. "Tak' this, too," he said, speaking thickly, while he handed over the money. "The wean brought its ain payment and mair—the wife and I are baith the better o't. The siller will maybe put up a bit sma' headstane. A' we want on't is the name. Though the wee thing wasna kirstened in an orthodox wye, it has a name, and under the name just put in—it'll maybe catch the e'e o' some that think different frae me—'Of such is the kingdom of heaven.'"

CHAPTER X.

DR. GEBBIE.

Had Matha Spale, the cartwright, and Peter Shule, the betheral, been wholly dependent on the making of coffins on the one hand, and the digging of graves on the other, their occupation would have been comparatively light—for Glenbuckie, as a parish, held a good place amongst the parishes of Scotland in point of mortality. Fortunately for these individuals, the occupations just referred to were incidental factors in a general business. To be just, it is only fair to say, that Dr. Gebbie had some small share in the maintenance of this light death-rate. He was reckoned to be a man of great skill in his profession, and though the betheral dared to remark that "it didna pay him to let his patients under the grun'," this sinister insinuation was as untrue as it was ungracious; for, while his practice was never large, it was generally admitted that no one could say, justly, that he ever kept a case unnecessarily long on hand for the sake of fees. The mercenary element in his nature was extremely small, and at no time was he so happy as when the sick-bill of the parish was low. Three things were dear to the doctor's heart—leisure, snuff, and the studious solitude of his own room. Socially, he was rather angular. His manner was abrupt and dreamy. His mind was full of odd speculations, which he seldom pursued sufficiently far to enable him to arrive at useful or definite conclusions. He did not seem to be capable of sustained investigation; some new light was always crossing his mental vision, leading him aside from the main thought of which he was in pursuit. Only in his profession was he practical and persistent. To his housekeeper he was a perpetual enigma. Ann Forgie, or Mistress Forgie, as she was called by courtesy, had kept house to him for fifteen years—indeed, ever since he came to Glenbuckie. She was a very respectable person, fairly well educated, an economical manager, and, in earlier days, must have been really handsome and good-looking. Some people said he ought to have married her. He was exceedingly careless of himself —inclined to be slovenly in his personal appearance— and those who took the trouble to consider his private concerns concluded that it would be to his own advantage to transfer her from the outer court of housekeeper to the inner circle of companion and wife. This thought had more than once been on his own mind, but it was never allowed to hold his undivided attention so long as to bear fruit. Once only had things seemed as if about to take practical shape. Indeed, on this occasion his intentions were unmistakable, not only to himself, but to Mrs. Forgie, who stood in his study, not far from him, with mysterious and unusual flutterings about her heart. He was slowly, and with apparent certainty, leading up to the point of making a proposal, but as fate would have it, he paused to take a pinch of snuff. These pauses, as Mrs. Forgie well knew, were almost invariably fatal to connected thinking. Nevertheless she stood her ground. She had really never seen him so "canty and jocose" before. There were many things she desired to do for him which maidenly reserve rendered impossible, so long as the present relationship subsisted. Was it possible that now, and at last, matters were coming right? There was, to be sure, this unfortunate pause, but perhaps he might be pondering how the important question should be stated to her, so she stood on, with a flushed face, waiting till he should break the fateful silence.

"Mrs. Forgie," he said at last, very gravely wiping the particles of snuff from his upper lip. "Do you think the planets are inhabited?"

"Eh, doctor, how do ye think I should ken whether the planets are inhabited or no?" she replied, thinking this was maybe a poetical way of treating the subject. She had read of such things in books.

"That's honest," he said heartily, "that's honest.

When one knows nothing about a thing, let him say so and be done with it. Dr. Chalmers speaks and writes sensibly on astronomy, I'll admit, for he knows what he's talking and writing about; but I have learned from William Dickie that your minister, Mr. M'Whinnie, has been following in the same line—that, in fact, he indulged last Sunday in the absurd sentiment that the stars were peopled with myriads of human beings like ourselves. If he had said spirits there might have been some reasonableness in the remark—but human beings! Mrs. Forgie, the thing is preposterous. I say the thing is preposterous. Let us take the planet Neptune, for instance, which is more than 2600 millions of miles further from the sun than we are, and I ask you, will any sane person say that the temperature in that planet is such as to maintain human life?"

It was clear the "bogie" had again crossed his path, and he had followed it. Poor Mrs. Forgie went back to her duties feeling humbled and downcast. What right had she to dream that the doctor's freedom of speech had its origin in any other feeling than that of confidence in her as his housekeeper? She was discontented and unhappy, but she felt all the more miserable in the belief that she had been deceiving herself with a false hope. From his earliest days Dr. Gebbie had been of a curt and cynical manner. He hated sentiment. Before coming to Glenbuckie he had been medical superintendent of the blind asylum in a large town in the north. There was a committee of lady visitors attached to the institution which gave him more trouble than the whole board of management. On this committee there was a lady who, in season and out of season, vexed and worried him with sentimental prattle and interference. One day, happening to come across the doctor in an "uncanny" mood, she inquired innocently enough whether blind people ever married.

"To be sure they marry," replied the doctor, rather tartly.

"Poor creatures! And do they have children?"

"Always," he retorted, with dangerous promptitude.

"Now just think of that," said the matron. "And do the children see?"

"Not a stime, they are all as blind as bats." While the tender-hearted sentimentalist was trying to grasp this astounding physiological phenomenon the doctor turned suddenly and said—

"Do you see that man sitting at the door there with the wooden legs? Well, that man's wife has five children and they have all wooden legs! It's simply a question of heredity."

This shameful outburst of cynicism not unjustly cost him his place. The committee of ladies took the matter up. They sat upon it, discussed it, magnified its rudeness, if that were possible, and ultimately so moved the minds of the directors, that the superintendent saw the only course left by which he might preserve his dignity was to tender his resignation.

The social life of Glenbuckie was not such as to make his disposition sweeter, or less reserved. At best there were but few with whom he could associate on anything like terms of equality. Dr. Plunket, the former minister, and John Humpleback, the schoolmaster, were as angular and full of peculiarities as himself. The one was shut up in that stern dignity peculiar to ecclesiastics of the period, who felt the necessity of holding a strict rein on a church prone to "divisive courses;" while the other was soured by the ever-encompassing sense of failure. Dr. Plunket and the schoolmaster, however, both passed away, and though their successors had entered into their labours, there was no particular, social, or sympathetic bond allowed to grow up between them, for in truth the doctor's habits were too deep rooted to be easily changed. Perhaps the person who interested him most, and who exercised the greatest influence over him, was Robert Simpson. This personage was a constant mystery to him. They had been born under widely different stars. There was a freshness, a vivacity, a subtle, but kindly humour about Robert's manner and speech which fascinated while it puzzled him. Simpson, on the other hand, derived amusement from the doctor's odd ways. He ridiculed his peculiar views, inveighed against his eccentricities, and, by a process of banter peculiar to himself, did more to rescue the doctor from the perils of impending misanthropy than any one had ever done before. The doctor did not like politics, the subject required too much continuity of thought. He was soured at religious polemics because of the sectarian bigotry and unchristian bitterness which characterised the discussion of religious questions; but he was fond of discoursing on vague scientific and metaphysical speculations, which, if clear to his own mind, were in the expression of them often hazy enough to the listener.

"Are ye an entity or a nonentity?" he inquired of Robert Simpson, one night as the two sat together over a glass of toddy.

"Weel," said Simpson, somewhat startled by the unexpected character of the question, "for the sake o' peace, doctor, I'll admit I'm an entity."

"Wrong," cried the doctor, catching eagerly at the admission. He pulled out his snuff-box and took a deliberate pinch, twisted his red pocket-handkerchief into a string and laid it across his knees, repeating as he did so, " Wrong."

"Then what on earth are ye gaun to make o' me?" inquired the supposed entity, evidently prepared for some sacrifice.

"You are simply a link in a chain of circumstances."

Robert laid down his glass, and rose to his

feet, with an unfathomable expression on his face. "Doctor," he said, "in some respects you are a real decent fellow. Ye may even be a philosopher for a' I ken, but why, in the name o' friendship, should ye invite me here to partake o' your hospitality and insult me by starting a metaphysical argument for the purpose o' proving that I am simply a link in a chain o' circumstances?" The questioner's look, more than his words, demanded an explanation.

"My dear sir," said the philosopher, "do not take my words amiss. The case was hypothetical. We are all links in a sense. The word was not intended to be personal—it applies equally to the whole human family. Nature is responsible for it all. She takes an interest in us so long as we serve her purpose; but when we cease to do that, she lets us slip through her fingers without caring to know what may befall us." Robert sat down amused, if not instructed. This, he thought, might be an important question, and might concern philosophers, but as he was not a philosopher it need not concern him.

Some time after this event a message came to Simpson, saying the doctor was in great trouble, and wanted to see him without delay. Mrs. Forgie, it appeared, had given up her place. She had received a letter from a cousin in Aberdeen suggesting that she should come and live with her. This cousin was said to possess ample means, and as they were both lone women, it was urged they would both be more comfortable together than living apart. Mrs. Forgie had thought over the proposal for several weeks before mentioning the matter to her master. It was years since they had seen each other. Her chief recollections of Miss Semple were that, as a girl, she was rather exacting and selfish, but in the years that intervened there had been much trouble, and this, no doubt, had worked changes in her disposition; at all events, they were relations—a change might be good for all parties—so, that afternoon, she gave formal intimation to the doctor of her intention to leave his service. When Robert Simpson went down in the gloaming he found the doctor in his study, with several books of reference laid out before him. Some abstract question was evidently perplexing his mind. In fact, he was for the moment trying to account for the spots in the sun's surface by endeavouring to ascertain the physical constitution of the sun itself. "There is no end to their theories," he said, shutting one of the volumes with a snap. "It appears to me on the hypothesis here laid down that a facula is a portion of luminous matter which has been removed high up into the atmosph——" he suddenly paused, for his visitor, who had stood at the open door for some seconds, with the corners of his mouth well elevated, now advanced a step into the room, and caught the doctor's eye.

"Come in, sir, come in; for I confess to you that I am in some difficulty regarding these remarkable phenomena. Would you believe it, sir, some of these theories are in direct opposition to established physical laws?"

"Very likely," said Simpson. "I have already called ye a philosopher, and I'll no withdraw the remark; but if you have sent for me to help ye out of a scientific difficulty that even philosophers themselves seem to differ about, a' I have to say about it is, that ye have sent for the wrong man."

"My dear sir," cried the doctor, his face suddenly assuming a look of real concern. "How stupid of me! In truth, this is not the object of my sending for you, and, to speak plainly, I want your advice very much, for I am in a condition of profound dejection. Mrs. Forgie, would you credit it, sir, who has lived under my roof for the last fifteen years, and who has made herself in some sense indispensable to me, has given up her situation."

"That is a spot i' the sun, truly."

"Yes," cried the doctor, waxing more vehement as the impending personal trouble gained fuller possession of his mind. "Was there ever anything like it? Did you ever hear anything so absurd? My dear sir, they talk about reforming the laws— but why do they not frame laws to make indispensable housekeepers stick to their places? I am truly in great trouble, and I would be sincerely thankful if you could tell me what I am to do to avert this disruption." The climax of his quandary having been reached, he leant helplessly back in his chair and began to finger his snuff-box in great agitation. His counsellor, meantime, sat gazing into the fire, with the look of one who had been equally crushed by the melancholy tidings. " Where is she going ? " he inquired by and by.

" To some lunatic of a cousin in Aberdeen, or some place; the thing is so absurd—so unreasonable."

" Yes," said Simpson gravely. " I 'm no surprised that Mrs. Forgie should want a change. Fifteen years' faithful service without promotion is a long time. Ye talk about reforming the laws, doctor, to suit your case, but that 's no needed ; there is a gey auld law in existence already that would serve ye weel enough, and if you will only apply it, I 'll be surprised if Mrs. Forgie ever leaves Glenbuckie."

" Good," cried the doctor gleefully. " What law ? "

" The law of marriage. Mrs. Forgie is a decent, discreet, and virtuous woman, and would make a thrifty wife."

Dr. Gebbie looked thoughtful for some seconds before he replied.

" Well," he said, with a sigh, " I have sometimes thought I should have offered her marriage ; in fact, I nearly did so once or twice, but something always came in the way. Perhaps it is not yet too late—

stay, I will touch the bell, we might see if that would alter her determination."

"Not *we*," said Simpson, rising. "Ye canna ask a delicate question like that in such a blunt and business-like way. No woman who has any respect for herself would stand that. The fact is, doctor, ye canna do without Mrs. Forgie, and I would strongly advise ye to let neither sun nor moon, stars nor comets, enter your head again, till ye have told her plainly that ye want her to be your wife."

"Well, in truth, I am willing to make some sacrifice——"

"No, no," interrupted Robert, "there maun be no sacrifices. If ye speak o' sacrifices, I'll no answer for the upshot. Say ye have long respected her—that, in short, to be plain, ye canna do without her."

"To be sure, to be sure, that I can truly say. Any change to me will be a sacrifice, you know, that is all I meant; but, after all, she may have her mind made up—in other words, she may refuse."

"Still there is a probability—every probability, I should say. Now, if you will take my advice, you will shut up these books. Yes, that's business-like; shut every other thought out of your mind. Bring Mrs. Forgie ben, have ae guid hour's courting, wind up wi' a proposal of marriage, and I'll be bound her cousin in Aberdeen will have no chance at all against ye."

The doctor rose with tears in his eyes.

"I will take your advice," he said, shaking his friend warmly by the hand; "I will take your advice. I am an old man—a stupid, crotchety old man, but really your words have inspired me with great courage."

Next morning Dr. Gebbie visited Simpson immediately after breakfast.

"Well?" inquired Robert, looking at the doctor's beaming face.

"My dear sir, how can I express my thanks to you for your timely advice? A wonderful change has come over Mrs. Forgie's mind. It has all turned out as you supposed. She wrote a line to her cousin, and afterwards—would you believe it, sir?—she helped me to find out a most satisfactory thing regarding the spots—to the effect, that if a spot be a hollow in the sun's surface, as we have reason to suppose, it is only necessary to believe that there has been a descending current of cold absorbing atmosphere to account for the want of luminosity. A spot may thus be produced by two currents—one ascending and carrying the hot luminous matter up, the other descending and carrying the cold atmosphere down——"

"Doctor," said Robert Simpson, interrupting him, "you're a decent fellow, and for once in your life ye have done the right thing; but ye may trust to this that the result was greatly owing to the state o' the Dadians at the time. Now, however, that the twa currents have come to understand each other, and are about to travel in the same direction, tak my word for it there will be fewer spots on the sun's surface, or my name's no Robert Simpson."

CHAPTER XI.

MAGGIE WINLESTRAE.

THEY had taken the head of her drowned lover out of her lap, and borne him hence to rest under the eyes of luxurious grief. In the moment of agony she was rudely thrust aside and forgotten. She was left there on the cold seashore with her double burden of grief and wrong. Two years before her widowed mother had been laid in the old churchyard beside the manse. A frail, good-looking, friendless girl, she had to face the world and seek employment. This she found with a genteel family in Ardrossan, but the tempter came with honeyed words and garish promises, and this was the upshot of it all. During the long months of suspense and apprehension through which she had passed, she frequently tried to persuade herself that it was all a dream—the fancy of a disordered brain; sometimes, also, she hoped that his friends would relent, or that he might shake off their influence and fulfil his promises and repair—so far as possible—the injury he had done; but the last fragment of these hopes had been rudely and for ever destroyed.

Gathering her wet plaid about her she rose hurriedly from the sand, and turned her back on the broken pieces of the vessel and cargo which strong hands were trying to drag from the devouring sea. In all that eager throng there was no one to cast a rope of help to this frail human wreck that struggled painfully over the wet beach, through rain and storm. Pressing her tiny burden more closely to her bosom, she hurried on towards the cliffs. The sea had taken all she lived for on earth, and why should it not have herself also? She was already an outcast, and no one would care to inquire what had become of her. She climbed up over the rocks, then creeping forward under cover of a protecting ledge, stood and saw the dark lines of sea-weed surging up and down in the seething caldron beneath her, and heard the deep boom of the waves, as they plunged into the caverns under the cliffs. One tottering step forward, and all would be over. She raised her head for a moment, and passed a wet hand over her burning brow. Were not these her mother's eyes that gazed down into hers with unutterable tenderness from the clear patch of azure above her? and were not these the sweet tones of the well-known voice calling to her from that other world, where, at their last parting, two years ago, they had solemnly trysted to meet?

She drew back in horror from the edge of the awful gulf, and fell trembling upon the wet rocks. Numbed with cold, and stupefied by the hopelessness of her misery, what could she do but sit there till the relief, which she had sinfully thought to hasten, gradually came? The wind blew in gusts from the sea, carrying with it occasional showers of spray from the great angry waves as they dashed themselves against the headlands, but already she was drenched to the skin, and it was no good seeking shelter from wind or spray. Her body and that of her child would be all the more readily discovered where she was, and, perhaps, some one might lay them beside her mother in the old kirkyard beyond the hill. While these reflections were passing through her mind, a hand was laid tenderly on her shoulder, and some one pronounced her name. She opened her eyes, and gazed up wildly at the kindly face that was looking compassionately into hers. It was a face which itself bore traces of disappointment and suffering, but the disappointments sprung from a different cause, and found their source in the political misrule of a great but down-trodden country —it was Jamie Pinkie, radical and tailor.

"Come, Maggie," he said, "come, lass, ye maunna sit there in the wind and rain, and get your death o' cauld on a day like this. Lord, bless us," he continued, passing his hand over her wet plaid, "ye're just soakin'! Get up, woman, and I'll gie ye a hand to some place o' shelter where ye can get yersel' dried."

"A' doors are shut against me," she said. "I'm owre bad to be taken in by onybody." She hid her pale face in her plaid and cried bitterly.

"I'm sure ye're no that much to blame," said Jamie soothingly. "Ye have been geyan ill-used ae wye and anither by them that should have been prood o' ye; but, come awa', what's the use o' us arguing aboot it, when ye're in such a sad pickle? We hinna muckle to brag o' at hame, but there's at least ae door open for ye. There's my sister Jean, she's as kind a being as ever breathed the breath o' life. Ye may just tell yer troubles to her, for she kens a guid deal aboot women-folk, and has some skill o' weans too. At ony rate, ye maun just come awa' hame wi' me and get yersel' driet." Jamie took her by the arm and led her carefully over the rocks. "Ye'll let me carry the wee thing for ye. No? Well, I'll no insist, though I could do't well enough, and ye would gang a' the lichter for it."

Maggie had recovered somewhat before she reached the tailor's house. Jamie met his sister at the door, and after one or two silent facial movements on his part, his sister had a thorough apprehension of the case.

"Come awa'," she said sympathetically, "I have a guid, warm fire for ye, and ye maun just gie me the wean and I'll toast its taes, for I'm sure it'll be baith cauld and wet."

Then, turning to her brother, she said, "Did ye get doon to the wreck?" This was accompanied by other facial signs on her part, which Jamie well understood.

"No," he replied, "but I'm just gaun. Ye'll maybe no want me for an hour or twa, and if I should e'en bide three ye'll ken I have come by no harm."

Jamie and his sister had but a slight acquaintance of Maggie Winlestrae. They had heard of her misfortune, and they had heard also of the heroic manner in which she, single-handed, had borne the burden of her sin. Jean, whose heart was naturally tender, had frequently referred to the poor lassie's case, so that when attracted by the pale but pretty face on the seashore, and the touching despair of her remarks as to "all doors being closed against her," Jamie felt sure his sister would gladly take her in.

"Eh, but ye're sair wet, lassie," said Jean, when the women had got the house to themselves; "here's some o' my ain dry things for ye, and you'll gie me the wean till ye put them on."

Maggie sat down, put her head on the little bundle in her lap, and sobbed aloud.

"It's no use," she said; "it's no use, the wean's dead, and I wish I had died wi' it, for there's nothing to live for noo."

"Preserve us! surely it's no dead?"

"It's owre true!" said the mother bitterly, rocking herself to and fro in the loneliness of her grief.

Jean seized a blanket from the bed, spread the small form on her knee before the fire, and vainly endeavoured to impart animation to the frigid limbs. It was, indeed, too true—all her efforts were in vain, for the baby was dead!

Several weeks passed, and Maggie was still an inmate of this humble dwelling. She had recovered somewhat, but her increasing strength made it more painful for her to live on the labour of those who had already done so much for her in her helplessness. The brother and sister were not slow to mark this feeling, and they had privately talked the matter over.

"Ye tell me ye can flooer," said Jean, one day when they were alone. "Weel, my brother just wants ye to bide here—we have plenty o' room for ye if ye care to put up wi' us for a while. Flooering is geyan guid the noo; and when my cut is finished I'll ask the agent to gie me a web for you, and I'm sure we'll get on fine thegither, just working to each other's hand."

Maggie accepted this offer with much gratitude. How could she go out to service again and face the world with such a burden of sad memories? However much she might try to conceal it, would not her sin find her out and expose her to unkindly suspicions?

During the succeeding months she worked very hard at her sewing, and was seldom over the doorstep, unless when she took an occasional run out in the gloaming to spend a few meditative moments in the graveyard. Though pale and slender, she had recovered much of her natural beauty, but the quick, bright, merry buoyancy of earlier days had now given place to more sedate manners. She was very industrious, and when not sewing, always found some household duty to perform; and wherever she went, order and tidiness followed in her train. Indeed, the house had recently assumed quite a bright and attractive character, so much so that Jamie's habits had very much improved, finding, as he now did, sufficient comfort and enjoyment in his own home. Jamie was wont to attribute his improved habits to the passing of the Reform Bill, and to the fact that, at Nanse Tannock's, politics had given place to ecclesiastical wrangles, where, in fact, nothing was now heard but Intrusion and Non-intrusion controversies. Jean, however, knew better. She had a fairly keen insight into the thoughts and intents of her brother's heart, but like a wise woman held her tongue. During the long evenings they had many interesting conversations—perhaps conversations is hardly the proper word, for Jamie, as pleased him best, had most of the speaking to himself. He held forth to his heart's content on many subjects, while the women-folk listened to his often absurd and extravagant political harangues with exemplary patience. Maggie, in particular, had, or seemed to have, great power of endurance on such occasions; but in point of fact she was often pursuing reflections of her own, while Jamie, stimulated by the attention of his small audience, and by the quick flashes of his thoughts, threshed the truth out of the various subjects on which he discoursed to his entire satisfaction.

Once, after a long tirade on the social relations of the country, he was startled by an irrelevant question. Maggie, who had sat for half-an-hour gazing into the fire with large, dreamy eyes, turned to him and said suddenly—

"Jamie, what is marriage?"

The brother and sister were both amazed at this abrupt inquiry. Jean first looked at the dreamy inquirer and then at the small oracle who was now appealed to as an expounder of the law.

"Marriage," repeated Jamie, pronouncing the word slowly, with the view of gaining time to frame a definition which would not hurt her feelings. "Marriage," he said, "is the union o' twa hearts that are drawn thegither by mutual sympathy, withoot ony pressure frae the ootside."

Jamie paused for a moment. He thought he had maybe said enough.

"Is that a' that's needed?" she inquired.

"In the eyes o' Heaven, yes," he said; "but inasmuch as man canna see into human hearts, the law demands some outward token. But, in spite o' ministers and magistrates, some folk that gang through the ootward form o' the thing are in the truer and higher sense o' the word no married ava'."

Jamie thought there might be some consolation to the inquirer in thus qualifying the legal aspects of the question.

Maggie did not seem to desire further discussion of the subject, so, for the present, it was allowed to drop. Jamie's growing attention to work, and improved sobriety of habits, became more and more marked every day; indeed, he was rarely out of doors at night now. As soon as the labours of the day were over, he would take the arm-chair in the ingle nook, for which Maggie, with her own fingers, had made an embroidered cushion, and there he would sit reading the newspapers—for newspapers were in vogue now—discoursing on the topics of the time; or, as frequently happened, he would sit for long periods simply watching the bonny face and nimble fingers of Maggie Winlestrae, as she sat near him, flowering her web, or shaping some useful knickknack for the good of the house.

Jean thought he had become painfully sober, and would not have been sorry to see him taking a little outing now and again, for he was beginning to look pale, and she was afraid such persistent virtue might tend to injure his health. She was revolving these thoughts in her mind one day when Jamie jumped suddenly off the board and followed her ben the house.

"Are ye ill, Jamie?" she inquired in alarm, as she beheld the excited little form before her, with the pale face.

"Dod, I'm ill, Jean," he replied decisively, shutting the door.

"Mercy! will I rin for Dr. Gebbie?"

"Ye needna fash about the doctor," he said, "it's a gey auld trouble—but I have tholed, Jean, till I can thole no longer. I maun speak."

"To be sure," she said, seizing a corner of her apron and commencing to crimp it nervously. Her suspicions were confirmed; she saw what was the matter.

Now that it had come to the point, Jamie observed there were delicate issues involved, about which he found it difficult to speak, and in the pause which ensued his sister relieved him.

"It'll maybe be easier for ye if I speak first," she said. "I ken what ye are going to say—ye would like to mak' Maggie Winlestrae your wife."

Jamie seized his sister's hand and pressed it gratefully before he could reply.

"But it'll mak' no change wi' you, Jean," he said. This was the point he wished to put straight. "We'll live on thegither just as before. I think you and Maggie will get on braw and weel, and I canna bide to think o' her maybe gaun awa' some day and leaving us a'thegither."

"I'm willing to risk it," said his sister bravely; "but have ye asked hersel'?"

"Not yet—have ye ony fear?"

"I'm no so sure," she said, "but I'll gang oot a message in the gloaming, if ye like, and ye can speir hersel'."

CHAPTER XII.

THE MINISTER'S RECORD (*continued*).

BEYOND dispute we live in times of great change. The social and material fabric of our lives seems to be taking on a different pattern, so to speak. It truly behoves thoughtful men to sit down, and look all this social, religious, and political ferment in the face, and consider what it is tending to. My book has suffered sorely from these causes, for to encompass the labour of writing a successful literary work, one must possess a settled mind, and be free from the harassments, or as one may say, the carking worries which are too prone to break in upon one's solitude from without.

What would our grandfathers think? We are now getting our carding, spinning, weaving, and sundry agricultural operations done by that great agent, steam; and as if that were not enough, we are threatened with having even our peaceful meadows and lovely glens mutilated by the running of steam-coaches over a track laid down with iron rails. This will no doubt be a wonderful thing to see—for my wife tells me these steam-trains run at an awsome rate of speed. I am sure I know not how they will be looked upon by the beasts of the field, who will stand in great danger of bodily harm; and not only so, but as Haplands was hearing from some one, the kye, who are such timorous creatures, may go back in their milk with fear, and so, serious hurt may be done to the farming interests of the country. Robert Simpson, who is much given to the reading of newspapers, informs me that the Railway Bill has passed through both Houses of Parliament, and that already, civil engineers have been seen traversing the land, with their yard-sticks and measuring-tapes, preparatory to laying down the metal rails on which the carriages are to run. Well, all these things have an unsettling effect on the minds of my people. As I jaloused at the time, the Reform Bill, which has now become the law of the land, has whetted their appetite for further novelties, and nothing will do but the Kirk itself must go through certain ordeals of mutation. The Evangelical party, as they call themselves, in their zeal for what is termed the rights of the people, have raised burning questions in our Church Courts, which, if not extinguished by a higher Hand, may scorch not only their own fingers, but do grievous damage to the Church itself. The people, not the patrons, are to be masters now. A majority of the male heads of families are to have liberty, or as it may more accurately be termed, licence to reject the nominee of the patron without any reasons given or required. This is what they call the Veto or Non-intrusion Act. As to chapels-of-ease, the question does not fash me much, one way or other, for there is little fear of any such chapel being set up in Glenbuckie. It is a right and proper thing that these charges should be given to the younger men, who ought to learn to work under experienced and trained parish ministers before they are allowed to rule. But the so-called Evangelicals wish to invest the chapel ministers with the power of ruling, and with the dignity of sitting in the Upper Courts, with the view, as it seems to me, of augmenting their own numbers, and increasing the vote against the more moderate members of the Assembly in carrying through their destructive and radical measures of reform. A few weeks ago I was waited upon by a deputation of parishioners, including some of my own elders, and invited to deliver an address on the subjects at present agitating the public mind of the country; but as I was in no way inclined to commit myself, and as I had no wish to stir up or keep alive party spirit, I advised them to go home and mind their own concerns, and let well-enough alone. This answer, I fear, was not taken in good part, for what did they do but invite a chapel minister from Beith to come and address them? It was a most painful and vexatious thing, and one, I believe, without precedent, that a chapel minister should come into the parish, and address a meeting without the parish minister's consent being first asked and obtained. I trust it is permissible to " be angry and sin not,"— at any rate the thing put me in a sore temper; but when I proposed to have the ringleaders of the movement brought under discipline, there was such a *fracaw* in the session that I had to give way for the sake of peace, and let the matter slip as easily as I could.

Thanks to the Father of Mercies, the twin-children are well, and are thriving into as bonnie bairns as you could clap eyes on. They are now running about as frisky as March hares. They have both emerged from the horrors of that painful scourge whooping-cough, which is indeed a merciful deliverance; but for the complete healing of the disease, we had to remove to the salt water at Irvine, and there we sojourned a month and a day. Mrs. M'Whinnie was also greatly benefited thereby, which is a great comfort, for she is again in a critical condition of health. In spite of these family troubles, which I have jocularly laid at her door, she has been a great source of strength and comfort to me, and has given me heart in combating with the many difficulties of my parochial work.

While catechising in the landward part of the parish to-day, I must confess I got some droll answers. I should say that this district is, by distance, removed from the immediate oversight of the pastoral eye, and consequently cannot enjoy the same advantages of spiritual supervision and instruction as the members of the flock that are nearer at hand. They can hardly therefore have the same measure of responsibility. Tullochmains I always looked upon as a simple but godly man. Having laid my plans to reach the uttermost bounds of the parish, in which his farm is situated, before the season of holy communion, I bespoke a lift for the betheral on the post-cart this morning, for the body's not so souple as he used to be, being sorely afflicted at times with the rheumatics. The betheral had given due warning of my coming, according to custom. I got over in the afternoon and found all the servant-folk, male and female, dressed and seated in the kitchen. The laddies were eident at their Question Books, and Tullochmains himself sat in a corner with the cloth-covered Bible on his knee in a most reverent attitude. The line of interrogation started with the Covenant of Works, and then passed on in a most natural, and, I trust, edifying manner, into the inner or more spiritual ground of the Covenant of Grace—ending at the very citadel of the doctrine, with Adoption and Sanctification. Barring the two servant lasses, the young people seemed to have a fair share of Bible-knowledge, considering their opportunities; and even the ploughman, a rough harum-scarum kind of a lad, answered not that ill. I asked him if he thought his works would save him, and he replied, in an offhand manner, that he thought they would be "hurried enough." This ready reply on the part of the lad put me in mind of an answer I received from the orra man at William Dickie's before last spring sacrament. He seemed a gawky kind of a coof, and not like one who had great hold of Bible-truth. I was dealing with the doctrine of the Fall and its consequences, and asked him, in simple language, what kind of a man he considered Adam was. I did not expect much, but he gave a really surprising and natural answer. "Adam?" he said, coughing rather irreverently; "weel, I'm thinking Adam was just such another as Johnnie Gibbie the horse-couper."

"How so, my friend?" I inquired.

"Weel, sir, ye see, just this way: nobody ever got onything by him, and mony lost."

Before leaving the Mains it behoved me, as having the spiritual oversight of old as well as young, to address a few words to Tullochmains himself. The male heads of families are supposed from their responsible positions to have a good grip of the fundamentals, so I asked him what he thought of the doctrine of Total Depravity. He was rather slow to answer; but at last said, "It's a grand doctrine, sir; it's really a grand doctrine, gin a body could just live up to it." I cannot tell you how grieved I was at hearing such a reply, especially from a man of ripe years, and one having the paternal care of a growing family. Maybe he had misunderstood what I said, at all events I did not press the question further, but when I narrated the matter afterwards to my wife, solemn as the circumstances were, she laughed, as it seemed to me, with almost irreverent heartiness.

Before closing this chapter of my record perhaps I should refer to the case of honest John Humpleback, the late schoolmaster and session-clerk. It is now some time since John passed away. He was a dominie of the old school, so to speak, who had taken to parish teaching because most other things had failed him. He was bred to the ministry, and truly he had great store of Latin and Greek, and was wonderfully versed in the different phases of mental and natural philosophy. I never heard it once hinted that he was defective in life, literature, or doctrine, but he was said to be " dry " in his preaching, and as his person was somewhat misshapen, or as I might say, deformed, the people did not look upon him with favour. It is true he was presented, as he has often told me, to the parish of Dundrumlie, on the southmost borders of Ayrshire, but after twice preaching in the vacant charge there arose such a sough of opposition among the parishioners as, I am told, has seldom been equalled in the history of disputed settlements. John Humpleback, however, was a dour man when he was crossed. His appeal to the Presbytery was lost; but when it came before the General Assembly, after two days' hearing of evidence, that august Court found that the main objections resolved themselves into this, that the presentee had a red head of hair, and was somewhat misshapen about the shoulders. They accordingly sustained the appeal, and remitted the matter back to the Presbytery, with instructions to their Riding Committee, as it was called, to see the appellant duly collated as minister of the parish of Dundrumlie. I am told the scenes in the parish were something awful to behold. The people were clean mad, at what they considered an attempt to ride rough-shod over their consciences, and they behaved in a most unbecoming, not to say ungodly fashion. Two separate attempts were made to proceed with the ordination, but in the first, the members of Presbytery either stayed away of their own accord, or were forcibly detained by the people, so that there was not a quorum of members present; and in the second, John Humpleback, as he told me himself, while on his way to the kirk, was seized stealthily by several of the parishioners, blindfolded, and carried to a neighbouring change-house, where, under pain of cruel bodily chastisement, he was compelled to drink the health of the more popular candidate, and swear to renounce all claims to both the temporal and spiritual privileges of the charge. It was verily a cruel and hard cross to bear, and his spirit was sore crushed down within him; but it so happened that a vacancy occurred in the Glenbuckie parish school about the same time, and Dr. Plunket having taken a liking to the man from his deportment in the Assembly, he used great influence amongst the heritors on his behalf, and got him the appointment. Now that he has passed away, I may safely say he was a worthy, albeit a sourish person, but from his knowledge of ecclesiastical forms and Church law, he was a great help to me in the conduct of the business of the session.

His place has been filled by a much younger man, from Johnstone, named Malcolm M'Crindle, also college-bred. He was carried into the appointment rather against my will, for, I would fain have had an older man, who was a fellow-student with me in the Divinity Hall in Edinburgh; but, after all, he is doing the work not that ill. My main objection to him is that he is of a light, or I might say, frivolous turn of mind, and writes poetry, a kind of literature I have no respect for myself, as it does not seem to me compatible with the more serious duty of training the young; but, strange to say, my wife is wonderfully taken with him and his works. She brought a copy of *Tait's Edinburgh Magazine* into my study the other day—where she got it I cannot say —doubtless it was from the lad himself, and she showed me a whole page of rhyme, entitled "A Lark's Matin." The thing had taken her fancy somehow; but as for me, I could make neither head nor tail of it; truly, there is no accounting for tastes.

PART FOURTH

CHAPTER XIII.

JAMIE PINKIE MAKES A PROPOSAL.

As arranged, Jean Pinkie went out in the gloaming, and left her brother and Maggie Winlestrae all by themselves. Maggie had her head bent intently over a muslin chemisette, on which the white flowers slowly blossomed in response to the touch of the flying needle. The work, while artistic in itself, was so far mechanical as to leave the mind free for other thoughts, and to judge by the pale and meditative look on the girl's face, it was evident she was not thinking of her immediate surroundings. Jean used to say to her brother sometimes when watching the large dreamy eyes set upon some object, such as the fire, with the sight turned inwards, "Maggie's no here," or, "She's no in," then Maggie, startled by the sound of her name, would break off her reverie, and repay the sympathetic brother and sister with a gentle apologetic smile.

On this occasion, Jamie saw clearly enough that Maggie "wasna' in." Nevertheless, he leapt from amongst his shapes and cuttings as gently as he could, and, coughing several times, as if he had caught his death of cold, he planted himself down at her side. Maggie suddenly awoke from her dream, and gazed at him with a sad, but rather wistful smile. He took the "hoops," which stretched the muslin, gently out of her hand, and sat for some little time contemplating the small sprig of buds and dots which she had been sewing. Maggie watched him with a pleased look, for she was accustomed to his appreciative curiosity now. He often stood near her watching the deft needle heaping its shining sprays upon the gauzy cloth; and not unfrequently would he take the work out of her slender hands, and remark upon her skill, but never had he done so before with such unspeakable feelings surging in his breast.

"Maggie," he said, by and by, "I have come owre to speak to ye about something."

The girl opened her eyes wide, and looked dismayed. Was this long, sadly happy time also come to an end? She was burdensome to them, and now she must go. The thought pained her deeply. She herself ought to have taken the initiative, but they had been considerate, and she felt as if she had taken ungenerous advantage of this humble pair.

"Yes," she said, "I should have thought of it too; I will go away—ye have been owre kind to me."

"Go away!" he repeated, with a shadow on his

face. "Isn't that just what I said to my sister? I telt her ye would be going away some day."

"And so I will," she replied, rising.

"Maggie," he said, taking her nervously by the hand, "for God-sake sit still for a minute, and listen to me. I thought ye wouldna feel quite comfortable as ye are, but I wanted to gi'e ye a better footing in the house. My sister and I have talked the thing owre between oursel's, and it's quite feasable, Maggie, I want to marry ye." Jamie took the girl's two burning hands in his, and watched the great warm tears flowing down the averted face. Jamie thought it would be better to let them flow, for a while, so he waited patiently and did not speak. "My sister will be real weel pleased if ye'll marry me," he ventured, when the little storm was over.

"Oh no, no," she said; "we must not think of that—you said I was married already, by your explanation of what marriage is."

"To be sure, and so ye were to a' intents and purposes," said Jamie consolingly; "but—but—" How should he put it? "Ye are left a' by yer lane now, and—" What was this he had done? He had wounded the gentle spirit he so anxiously strove to spare. Poor Maggie hid her face in her apron and sobbed aloud.

"Wheest," he said, "wheest, Maggie lass, ye maunna give wye like that, I didna ettle to hurt ye. We canna bring back them that's awa', and

I'm sure I'll do everything I can to make ye comfortable."

"You have been owre kind to me already," she sobbed—"far owre kind. Oh, ye maunna ask me to do that."

Had she spoken out the thoughts in her mind at the moment, she would have told him how such a proposal jarred on her feelings. A widow, as she now supposed herself, of but six months' standing, her heart still belonged to her first love; her hope was, that no obstacle should ever come between them till they met again. "Jamie," she said, looking at him with a sad tenderness, "ye have been kinder nor ony brother to me. Ye saved my life, and ye have helped me to bear what, without the sympathy of yer sister and yersel', would have been unbearable. It would be nice to go on this wye just as we are— but I canna—oh, Jamie, I didna think o' this,— dinna ask me—for I'm no guid enough for ye."

"Guid enough!" shouted Jamie, getting to his feet, "ye're guid enough for the best man in the land, let abee a puir tailor body like me; but though I hinna muckle to offer ye, I'm willing to lay in till the wark—I have wasted a guid heap o' time, I'll admit, on an ungrateful country, but, Maggie, ye have dune me mair guid than 'Reform' and the 'Rights o' Man' baith put thegither. I must confess to ye that these subjects never acted so powerful in takin' me oot o' the hoose as ye have done in keeping me in; and I'm sure if I work the wye I have been doing since ye cam' to bide with us, we micht sune be as comfortable as if the Embro Parliament had been an established fact. I must say ye're the best embodiment o' Reform that ever crossed my door. Weel, so much on that score. Now come, Maggie lass, is it to be a bargain? Dinna look so sad about it, for I canna bide the thought o' ye ever going away from us."

"You pity me," she said mournfully. "You want to be kind because ye are sorry for me———"

"Pity's no word for't ava," interrupted Jamie. "I'm fair daft aboot ye; Jean kens I am. I can neither eat nor sleep for thinking on ye; and it was my sister hersel' that urged me to tell ye aboot it."

Poor Maggie was driven into a corner. From her inmost heart she respected the hospitable little man before her; she had never dreamed, however, that he wished to be more to her than a protector and a friend. He was worthy of love. He was worthy of the devotion and self-abnegation of a life; but what had she to give him? She, whose heart had only six months ago been buried in the grave with her first and only love. She dare not look him in the face; she could never give him a proper return for what he had offered her—what then could she offer him but bitter tears of penitence and regret?

Jamie could stand anything but tears.

"Maggie," he said, "maybe I have been owre rough wi' ye—maybe I have spoken owre soon———"

"Oh," she sobbed, "if I could tell ye—if ye only kent how I feel."

"I think I ken," said Jamie tenderly. "Will ye be able to give me an answer in six months' time? We can stick in to the wark and gether a wee—will ye bide on wi' us on that condition, Maggie?"

"Yes," she replied, "if ye will let me."

"A' that I ask now is your promise never to marry another man."

"I will never marry another man," she said solemnly.

"Then a bargain's a bargain," Jamie said, taking her hand and pressing it respectfully to his lips. "Cheer up, my lass, we understand each other now." Maggie was respited, and she settled down to her duties in the old earnest and humble spirit. Six months would bring changes, she thought. At any rate it was a long while to look forward to. When Jean returned there was no evidence that anything had happened, save that Maggie's eyes were red and her face a trifle paler than usual, and Jamie was more earnest at his work. Jamie subsequently told his sister the result of his interview, and indulged in the belief that when Maggie had completed her twelve months of widowhood, she would become his wife. He had her promise, however, that she would never marry any other man.

Summer passed lightly; autumn came scattering his brown leaves in the misty lanes; then from the doors of Glenbuckie it might be seen that winter had thrown his snowy mantle over the Arran hills. All this time, Maggie had been silent and sad. She worked faithfully at her sewing; and when she changed her occupation it was only to perform some duty that added new attractions to the tailor's home. She seldom went to the graveyard now. Jamie had purchased a modest " headstone " and placed it over her baby's grave ; he had also procured a couple of dwarf yew-trees—these he had set, one at the head and the other at the foot of the little lair, and on the outside he had planted a soft border of summer snow. His sister was touched by these suggestive acts of tenderness ; and the feeling in her mind was deepened by the knowledge that Maggie Winlestrae would never become his wife. Her sympathetic eye and sisterly nearness to the unfortunate girl enabled her to make discoveries which had entirely escaped her brother's observations.

For months past, Maggie had gradually been failing in health, and, while, to the eye of her lover, her form was becoming more charmingly graceful, and her face more beautiful, Jean well knew what such grace and beauty portended.

Maggie had frequently been remonstrated with about her close attention to work, and urged, in a motherly fashion, to stir about and take more fresh air, but her reply on these occasions was generally a languid smile betokening gratitude for the sympathy which prompted such kind suggestions, and conveying her impression that the measures proposed could prove of but little avail. Toward the end of October, Jamie Pinkie began to discover in Maggie's frequent absence from their humble breakfast-table in the kitchen that all was not well—these were but preparatory monitions. Maggie gradually grew worse, and was by and by permanently laid aside. Jamie hoped for some time against hope. When his work was done in the evening he used to relieve his sister, who had her duties to perform in the kitchen, taking his place by the bedside, and administering the medicines which the doctor had prescribed. Everything in the shape of remedy that could be devised he was careful to procure, but it soon became, even to him, painfully apparent that no improvement resulted from these attentions. One evening while they were together, alone, Maggie looked at him with her usual placid smile, and said gently, "I'm gieing ye a heap o' trouble, Jamie."

Jamie rose with a mistiness in his eyes, went over to the bed, and took the thin white hand which lay on the coverlet. "Dinna talk about the trouble," he said, trying to speak bravely, but his voice failed him.

"I have asked your sister to let us speak a wee together, the nicht," she said by and by, with a strange light in her large eyes. "I hinna forgot what we promised to ane anither. It is six months since, the nicht; but I kent ye were owre kind to mind me o't."

"But the doctor said ye werena to speak, or fash yoursel' wi' onything," stammered Jamie.

"It canna mak' much odds," she replied. "There seems a strange spell about our tryst, Jamie, and something tells me I should speak to ye the nicht —ye winna be angry with me?"

Jamie could not reply, but he pressed the white hand which he still held.

"I canna tell ye how I respect ye," she said, after a brief pause. "Ye have been so gentle and brotherly wi' me, and I have been a heap o' trouble to ye——"

"Don't speak about that," interrupted Jamie. "I'm no so guid as ye mak' oot; but if I'm better than I ance was, it's you that has made me what I am."

"Weel," she continued, "it's a' true and mair, what I have said aboot ye. If I had been spared we micht a been married, but ye're no to be vexed for that. I saw it wasna to be, and noo when the time has come round for me to gie ye the answer, I can only bid ye good-bye." She could not proceed, for Jamie had hid his face in his hands and was sobbing bitterly.

"Dinna vex yersel'," she said gently. "I canna greet mysel', for I ken it's a' for the best, and ye'll see it that wye too. When a' this is by, we'll think kindly o' ane another, Jamie. I have been wayward and silly, but I have tried to be honest and true; and maybe, when I'm awa', ye'll think that though I brought a heap o' trouble on mysel' and ither folk, I meant no that ill."

When his sister came in, Jamie was kneeling at the bedside with his face buried in the bed-clothes.

"Come," she said, laying her hand gently on his shoulder, "ye maunna gie wye like that; Maggie is wearied, and ye maun let her get rest. I am sure ye are needin' a rest yersel', so if ye'll just say guid-nicht and gang to yer bed, it'll be better for ye baith."

Jamie rose to his feet, dazed and stunned, but Maggie held out her frail hand to steady him; while they clasped hands their eyes met in one long, full, eloquent gaze. Who can tell what passed between them then? There was a perfect understanding expressed in that look, and there remained no need for articulate farewells. Jamie stooped down and imprinted a burning kiss upon her cheek. It was the first and only time he had ever kissed her. It was also the last, for in the stillness of the autumn midnight, the spirit of Maggie Winlestrae passed away.

CHAPTER XIV.

MYSIE SHAW, THE SPAEWIFE.

ABOUT a quarter of a mile above the manse, and not far from the old post-road to Ayr, there was a curious little hovel, built mainly of turf and clay, against the face of a rock; the sloping roof was thatched with heather and brackens; there was an aperture in the upper part of this covering, surmounted by a blackened firkin, which served as a chimney, and, from a cross-beam immediately below, a chain depended, with the links rendered invisible by a thick coating of soot and dust. This chain had a movable crook at the lower end, and was suspended over a peat fire, in the middle of the floor. There was no window in the apartment, and the only passages by which light could enter were the firkin and the door; between these openings the smoke swayed and swithered with confused uncertainty—small whiffs now going this way and now that, while the bulk of it, having little persistent encouragement to take either course, remained inside. Here lived spae-Mysie and her son Tow. Tow, or

Thomas, as he had at one time been named, was an uncouth, dwarf-like, misshapen creature, who might have been taken for a boy of ten, but whose real age was twenty-five. Tow could not speak, but he had a peculiar weird language of guttural sounds, which, to his mother, was quite as intelligible as speech. Between these two a touching sympathy existed. Mysie seldom spaed a fortune without consulting her son. If his view differed from hers, the process was repeated, and, not until they could see eye to eye, was the fortune declared. For many years Mysie and her mate, a drunken tinker, had strolled about the country, pitching their tent now here, now there, and earning—for they were never known to beg—a precarious living; but on the death of her male companion, who was killed in a smuggling exploit, she came to Glenbuckie and settled down in one of their old haunts, a description of which is given in the opening sentences of this chapter. Both Tow and his mother were supposed to be gifted with second sight. Mysie was not, however, a mercenary diviner. While numerous timid maidens and amorous swains came to the "spaewife" seeking glimpses into the future, many of them were sent away, their offerings unaccepted, and their fortunes unread. She would not invent a future where, to her mind, no future was revealed. On the other hand, she did not fail to convey warnings, even when they were unsought. These voluntary visits were always dreaded—for they generally foreboded evil. By the young especially, Mysie was greatly feared. Many a child had its yaummering or sleepy cry hushed by the mention of her name; and in many a youthful dream the awsome form was found in hot pursuit, while willing legs were unable to obey the desire to run. Mother and son were seldom seen together, unless at home. They roamed abroad a good deal, but always separately. Tow avoided human society—his favourite haunts were in deep glens, where might be heard the eerie gurgle of rapid streams, or the murmur of waterfalls. The noise of water in agitation had a peculiar fascination for him: now, he might be seen pacing the uneven banks of the river, his eyes bent on the ground, and his arms clasped behind his back, or now, clinging, cat-like, to the rocks in the neighbourhood of a cataract far up the glen, in search of certain roots found in moist and sunless hollows for which, strangely, he had acquired a liking. When tired with these wanderings it was common to find him stretched on his back among tall brackens, where he would lie for hours, listening to the call of wood-pigeons or watching the squirrel performing its antics among the branches overhead.

One day the spaewife paid an unexpected and undesired visit to Marion Wilson at the Millstone Quarries. Marion was the grand-daughter of a farmer's widow in the parish, who had often afforded friendly shelter to Mysie and her mate in their earlier wanderings. Three months before, she was married to John Coultar, manager at the Quarries, and her grandmother had supplied her, amongst other things, with an excellent stock of home-spun linen. This embraced, as was customary in rural Scotland of the period, *dead-clothes* for herself and husband, and for the first time, the young wife had turned these things out of the chest where they had been stored, and, with becoming solemnity, proceeded to spread them before the fire to " air." Marion blessed herself, and nearly fainted as the uncanny visitor entered. What could this weird combination of circumstances signify but evil ? She had wondered to her husband the night before if ever anybody had been so happy as she had been since they were married. And then, as supreme happiness sometimes suggests the opposite by contrast, she burst into tears and feared she was " owre fond o' him, and didn't know what she would do if he was ta'en awa'."

" Air them weel," said Mysie, looking gravely at the articles so carefully laid out before the fire. " Guard them again' mildew, for the claes winna be needed for a while to come ; but, lass, there are waur troubles than daith, troubles that mak' us wish whiles that daith would happen. Last night I saw ye standing on the edge o' a deep mountain loch ; there was something oot in the water enticing ye to gang in. I saw your een dancing, as if ye were pleased wi' what ye saw, but what it was I canna tell ye. I ken it wasna your husband, for I saw him coming doon the hill behind ye in great haste, as if he wanted to reach ye in time. That's the riddle—but ye maun read it for yersel'."

Mysie's appearances and disappearances were as a rule equally abrupt. When she had a message to convey she would deliver it, but would not stay to be questioned. So, when Marion Wilson, who received this mysterious and probably fateful deliverance with bowed head, looked up to implore a fuller revelation, the spaewife had gone.

On Mysie's return home, Tow was found sitting in the smoke, with his head bent on his knees.

"My poor bairn," she cried, "my poor bairn; what is it noo?" He did not look up for some moments, but when he did there were great drops of perspiration on his face. She sat down beside him, so that his left foot touched hers—this was their method of seeing eye to eye. Tow raised his hands, and struggled as if in want of help, and gave utterance to some strange, unearthly, gurgling sounds.

"I see it," she said, "I see it; it is mair trouble. There is the minister, and there is mysel'. Guid kens, I have had plenty; but the trouble is for the minister and me, whatever it may be." Mysie laid her son's head gently on her lap, and began to rock herself to and fro, crooning the while a peculiar, weird tune. This was how she soothed Tow after these fits of divination. While they sat thus together, a heavy, uncouth foot was heard on the stones outside. After some fumbling about for the "sneck," the dim outline of a man was seen in the deepening twilight at the door.

"Are ye in, mistress?" inquired the intruder, stooping, and peering timidly through the smoke.

"Ay," she replied; "wha is 't that comes seeking guid news when there is so much trouble i' the air?"

"My name is Neebikin," said the visitor, "Richie Neebikin. I hear ye have unco skill in reading fortunes; but if there 's ony trouble, as ye say, in store for me, dod! it micht be as weel for me to bide till it comes. In troth, I 'm no heeding to hear it unless I can 'jouk, and let the jaw gang by.'"

"Just like the lave," she said absently. "Hurry on the joy, foretell only what is guid, but dinna lift the curtain frae the face o' pain. Come in, and sit doon here, till I see ye."

Richie moved forward in a sort of bewildered way. These references to trouble and pain rather upset him. What could they mean? Was the mistress going to put them on "neep" diet again? Richie and his mate, the cow-bailie at William Dickie's, had recently rebelled against the poverty of the feeding, and sturdily declined to take boiled turnips for supper every night, except Sunday.

They declared such diet was nothing better than a "blash o' bree," and "no fit for men either to work or sleep on." William endeavoured to soothe them by reading the sixth chapter of 1st Timothy, and laid stress upon the words, "They that have believing masters, let them not despise them."

"Believing masters!" said Richie's neighbour, speaking in the recklessness of a hungry rage; "Deevil tak' a wheen o' ye for scoudered heepocrites, sitting there lecturing about believing, when ye winna gie your servants their meat!"

This was admitted afterwards to be rather an injudicious remark; the diet, however, was improved, but the cow-bailie had to go at the next Martinmas term. After Mysie's words, Richie wondered if the mistress was going to "try it on again;" but the wrinkled seer stretched out her withered hand, and beckoned him to a stool at her feet.

"If the ill ye speak o' has ony relation to the mistress and me," Richie remarked, "maybe ye'll be as safe to let's hear it at ance; for I would as lief gang to the 'buchts' and seek anither place, as gang back again on a diet o' champit neeps."

Mysie was too busy scrutinising the full, well-coloured, healthy face of her uncouth client to pay much heed to these remarks.

"Ay," she said oracularly, "I see there's a lass in the case—a lass wi' gouden hair."

"Dod, an' ye're a gleg ane," cried Richie forgetfully. "So there is; just think o' ye kennin' that! —Weel, mistress?"

"Stick by your mother," continued the spaewoman. "I see ye have been braw and kind to her in the past. You will never rue that."

"But about Jeanie and me," inquired Richie, with impulsive indiscretion. "I mean the lass ye spoke o'. Weel, I needna try to hide onything, for ye ken a' the outs and ins o't. Am I likely to get her?"

"Jeanie is owre frolicsome for ye; she has a licht heart and licht ways. I canna see whether ye come thegither in the aftertime or no; but your mother is looking to ye for what help ye can gie, and I would advise ye, for the present, to stick to her."

Richie sauntered home, took his brose, and went to bed. He was not a rapid thinker at any time, but he lay awake till he had turned the matter over in his mind. He admitted that he was dutifully fond of his mother, but this lass had fairly captivated his fancy. She had such bonny een, and such hearty, winning manners; moreover, she lived in a house where there was a "guid rough kitchen," and it had been told him by no less an authority than the cow-bailie that she never was "sparing wi' the meat." Richie turned over on the other side, his drowsy pulses beating with a fine sense of pleasure. He would press forward beyond the line at which the spaewife had lost sight of them; who could tell but that, after all, she might marry him yet?

It was some days before Mysie Shaw had an interview with the minister. He was out one evening, pacing thoughtfully up and down in the bourtree avenue, putting some thoughts together which he considered suitable for his projected book on "Popular Social Sins," when suddenly a grim figure started apparently from among the grave-stones, pushed through the bushes, and boldly confronted him.

This sudden apparition occasioned him, as he said afterwards, "a sore and grievous shock to the nervous system. Nevertheless, faith triumphed over the fears of the imagination," and he was enabled to speak with "wonderful composure."

"May," he said, with gentle remonstrance, "why this nocturnal, and, I may add, unseasonable visitation? Why always come upon me thus in the gloaming? Is there anything you have to communicate that could not as well be said in the light of day?"

"The lark sings i' the sun," she replied, "because its song is a song of joy; but ill-tidings fa' fittest on the mind at mirk."

"Ill-tidings, said ye?" Neither his faith nor his education had been able to master that subtle drop of superstitious blood that now rushed to his brain, and tingled about the roots of his hair.

"Ay," she continued, "the ill I saw comes to me as weel as to you; there was something for each o' us; but mine was the darkest sorrow o' the twa." She paused and covered her face with her hands, as if trying to penetrate the mystery of impending evil. "Yours," she continued, "is not in your person, nor in your family, there is something wrong in the parish—it is coming on ye from without. Be on your guard. As for me—"—she threw up her arms as if struck violently by an unseen hand. Then she listened intently. "Didna ye hear that cry? Oh God! it was the cry o' my ain poor bairn." In a moment the minister was alone. Firmer nerves might have quaked under this weird encounter. He leant against the broken trunk of a tree to steady himself and regain composure. During the evening the atmosphere had been close and sultry, but, unperceived by him, the density had increased during this exciting interview, and now the sulphurous air seemed to catch fire from some mysterious light, and immediately overhead it hurtled and burst in appalling thunder. In the black stillness which preceded the rain, a wail came from the gorse and brackens above the manse, the burden of which was—" My bairn, my poor injured bairn!"

CHAPTER XV.

THE TEMPTER.

JOHN COULTAR, manager at the Millstone Quarries, was a hard-working, sober man. He had reached the position he occupied by the force of his character and the skill of his labour. He mixed little in the society of his fellows. There was a simple dignity in his manner which forbade undue familiarity, and which led some envious people to suppose that he thought himself "better than his neighbours." Indeed, Mrs. Macfarlane, the howdie, was heard one day to remark in confidential terms to a neighbour gossip that he reminded her "o' the sweep that stuck i' the lum—he was owre big for his place." John, however, was eager to get on, and he was determined to keep his standard up. The policy of dignified reserve, considering the social surroundings of his wife and himself, he believed to be both necessary and sound. The manager's cottage was situated about a gun-shot from the quarries. It stood all by itself on the bend of the hill above the village, and their nearest neighbour was this Mrs.

Macfarlane who had made the disparaging remark already referred to. The manager and his young wife had frequently talked over their plans and prospects. The period of their married life had as yet been brief, and, while he loved her very devotedly, he could discern that there was a want of firmness in her character, and a frank sociability of disposition, which made him, perhaps, over-solicitous about the making of her early friendships. This nearest neighbour he knew to be particularly aggressive; she was, moreover, a woman whose habits were very objectionable as an example to a simple und unsuspecting young wife, who had little or no experience of the world. Association with this person was his greatest fear. John circled again and again about the matter as delicately as he could, when his wife one day, grieved that he was making so much of it, said—

"Dear me, John, if the woman pays me a visit in a friendly way, am I to put her out?"

"No," replied he, firmly determined, since the thing had come aboveboard, to make his meaning quite plain; "but, Marion, if I were you, I wouldn't let her in."

Mrs. Coultar was turning the matter over subsequently, with a feeling of soreness in her mind that her husband should doubt her prudence, when the prohibited neighbour turned the handle of the door and walked boldly in. She was hearty and demonstrative, and at once commenced to talk with great familiarity. She had been up at Thrappledyke farm, as she took care to explain, engaged in the duties of her profession, for the past six weeks, which must be taken as her apology for not sooner calling to offer her respects and good wishes.

"Eh, what a trig kitchen ye keep!" she remarked, taking a good survey of the place after the preliminaries were over. "It's nice to see a young couple making sic a bien start i' the world. I was just saying this morning that I thought you and your man were a real happy couple—real happy. Ay; and do ye ken, when I see him lamping doun the hill, and you coming out on the door-step to meet him, wi' your blithe young face, it just puts me in mind o' the time when my ain puir man and me were marriet. . . . Oh but she was the proud limmer that wha leeved here before you, Mrs. Coultar—a proud limmer she was. I mind ae nurday I saw her polishing the brass plate on the door, and I ran up in a friendly wye to offer her a scent out o' our bottle, for, puir body, she was looking unco cauldlike for a nurday morning. So what do ye think my leddy will say, 'No, Mrs. Macfarlane,' says she, 'I'm no in the habit o' taking sperits on the public road, and it would be better if ye offered it to some person who is inclined to be more friendly wi' ye.' Oh, woman, I canna tell ye how muckle I was hurt. Sandy was living then, puir fellow, and was sitting at the fire-en' reading *Robinson Crusoe*—for he had an awfu' head for scientific and historical books—and when I told him what the woman had said, 'Serve ye richt,' says he, 'serve ye richt; if everybody had treated ye the same wye, guidwife, we 'd have been a richer couple the day.' Sandy kent weel how open-handed I was. Kindness is my fault, Mrs. Coultar. Kindness to my neighbours is ane o' the greatest faults I have. But, Mrs. Coultar, what's wrang wi' ye?" she continued, looking in the troubled face of the young wife. "Ye look unco feart-like for a bonny young marriet woman. He hasna been flyting on ye already?"

"Flyting!" said Mrs. Coultar, for the moment assuming a brisker air. "Oh no, it's too soon for that yet, Mrs. Macfarlane."

"Ah, lass, it's owre sune, but there's something troubling ye that ye shouldna hide. I have seen a hantle o' the world and maybe could help ye."

"Weel, it's just this," said Mrs. Coultar, stammering, but making a supreme essay at firmness. "You know my husband is very retired in his habits, and doesn't mind much for company, and I think, well, I rather think, he would like me to act very much as he does himsel'." How could she say more? It was impossible to show this woman to the door rudely, when she had come to pay her respects in such a frank and friendly way. Surely

John would not be angry with her, for had she not given as plain a hint in what she had just said as ordinary civility would allow?

"Oh ho, is that the wye o't?" cried the intruder, drawing in a seat to the fire and sitting down. "So you're no to be allowed to judge for yoursel'? It's a puir thing to be without neighbours, wi' him out among his ain kin' a' day lang. He canna lay doon the law for ye in your ain house surely? If ye let him do that, ye'll no have your sorrows to seek. My woman, ye have a heap to learn yet." She took a small bottle from under her apron, and lifting a cup which stood near her, poured out part of the contents, and offering it to the young wife, invited her to "tak' a drap o't for the sake o' friendliness. —What! ye winna taste it?"

"No, thank you."

"But, my lass, I'm anxious to be kind to ye, and this my first visit too! Tak' it i' your hand, and drink my health." Mrs. Coultar was shocked. Her first impulse was to take her husband's advice, and order the woman from her door; but she temporised. The interview, she thought, would come to an end, and why should there be an open rupture, when afterwards she could be on her guard?

"I would rather not," she said simply.

"Weel, here's my best respects to ye; the crack mak's a body dry. Heigh, heigh, it's an auld story noo, but I mind, sune after I was marriet mysel', the advice I got frae a decent neighbour woman that bade next door. She saw what a slave I was to my house, and she comes in and she says, says she, 'Noo, Mrs. Macfarlane, you're a young woman, and Sandy's a young man, and as ye begin wi' him, so ye maun gang on. I see it tak's ye maist a' day to have your house in order, and everything snod for him when he comes hame, and,' says she, ' he'll think, when he sees everything clean and never sees ye cleaning, that ye have nothing to do ava'. It's a' very weel,' says she, ' so lang as there's nothing hangin' on your hand, but my certie, lass, twa or three years 'll mak' a difference. Work 'll get heavier as ye gang on, but men mak' nae allowance for that. Noo,' says she, ' I'll put ye on a plan. Dinna you put a finger to your house till it's near time for him comin' hame, and have a'thing in disorder, and breinge and brattle about as if ye were slavin' yoursel' to death. Tell him the wark 's owre muckle for ye, that ye maun have a wee lassie to do the rough turns and rin your errands. Men are like ither folk, they can only see what's before their nose at the time. Do ye that, Mrs. Macfarlane, and ye'll have an easier time o't.' And so I had, honest woman."

"Did you manage to carry out your neighbour's plan?" ventured Mrs. Coultar, amused in spite of her displeasure at the suggestion of the tempter.

"Ay, but I took my ain wye o't. We had mony

a bit tussel at first. Some men are dourer than ithers, but even the dourest will give in at last if ye only keep at it. Sandy was no that ill to talk ower when ye kent the wye. In fact he was just ane o' thae easy-ozie kind o' men that would do onything for the sake o' peace. I mind ance, after I had fairly got the upper hand, he said it was ane o' the happiest recollections o' his life the first time he saw me. But, Mrs. Coultar, it's an unco cauldrife meeting, somehoo. Ye maun tak' a taste, woman, to put life in ye. It'll no do ye wan bit o' harm. Here na, put it to your lips, and say 'Here's to ye.'"

How could Marion resist such importunity and maintain good manners? She took the cup in her hand.

"That now, there's a leddy; tak' a sup o't. There's plenty for baith o' us, and it's no sociable-like to sit drinking a dram a' by yoursel'."

Mrs. Coultar simply put the liquor to her lips, and returned the cup, while her neighbour poured out the contents of the bottle, and quaffed it off, drinking to their "greater neighbourliness." "Whisky aye maks me grue, Mrs. Coultar; isn't that droll? I dinna think I would ever learn to be a drinker, for I never can tak' sperits but it maks me grue." Mrs. Macfarlane adjusted the ties of her cap, wet her fingers, caught up a dishevelled lock of iron-grey hair, and thrust it back into its place. "Weel, as I was saying, Sandy aye looket back wi' pleasure to that early time. There was a wheen lads and lassies o' us gathered thegither on the village green ahint John Armour's smiddy. Sandy was a gey strappin' chiel, and mony a braw lass had her e'e on him. Weel, ye see, we had fifes and fiddles a' playin' thegither, and we danced and better danced, up the back and doon the middle, crossed, joined hands, swung roun' aboot like peeries till our heads were soomin' and we were ready to fa' aff our feet. But after I had rested awee, and was putting my naepkin on to rin hame, he comes owre to me again. 'Janet,' says he, 'I want to have anither dance wi' ye, for I would rather have you than ony ither lass i' the company.' The thing cam out sudden and ramstam-like, but wearied and a' as I was, I cuist my naepkin to the winds. Sandy put his arm round my waist, and I put my hand on his shouther, and the fiddles played up Cocky-bendy." At this point, strangely enough, the narrator broke down, and gave way to tears. "Oh lass, lass, that was the dance! I never enjoyed onything half so weel. The lassies shaket themsel's, and the lads hooched and loupet, and whiles I think I hear that fiddle yet." . . . "Weel, woman, oot o' drink he was a guid man, and real easy managed." Mrs. Macfarlane lifted the empty bottle which stood on the kitchen table, shut one eye, and looked meditatively through it. "It was guid stuff that, Mrs. Coultar,—half a mutchkin o' the very best;

but, woman, half a mutchkin gangs nae length wi' twa folk." Mrs. Coultar simply concurred in this remark, and the bottle was laid down on the table again with a sigh. "But, as I was saying, Sandy sometimes took a gey heavy dram; and although I never allowed him to be masterfu', he was as cunning as a fox. I mind he got up ae Sunday morning unco dry, for he had been drinking heavy the night before.

"'Gie me a shilling,' says he, slipping owre to the bedside in his stocking-soles.

"''Deed, and I'll do no such thing,' says I, taking the wean in my arms, and turning my face to the wa'.

"'You'll no?' says he.

"'No,' says I firmly.

"'Aweel, then,' says he. So he gangs owre gently to the kitchen-press ayont the fire, while I had my back to him, and he tak's oot the bank-book. I had something saved, ye ken, for a rainy day—and awa' goes the man to Mr. Milroy, wha keepit the bank. 'Mr. Milroy,' says he, pretending to greet, and fingering the bank-book, 'my wife Janet's dead.'

"'Dead!' cried Mr. Milroy. 'When did that happen?' 'Yestreen,' said oor ane. 'It was awfu' sudden—and—and—I'm sorry to trouble ye on a Sunday morning.'

"'Don't name it,' says Mr. Milroy. 'You have

lost a guid wife, poor man. There 'll be some bits o' things wanted, no doubt.' So he puts his hand in his pocket, and gies him a pound-note right off, and telt him to come back in the morning, and he would get as much as would put me decently under the grund.' So what do ye think, Mrs. Coultar, but Mr. Milroy meets the lassie gaun to her work in the morning, and he says, 'What, are ye gaun to your work the day, my lassie?' 'Ay,' says she, kind o' donnert-like. ''Deed, I suppose it 'll be a' needed, puir bodies,' says Mr. Milroy, speaking like to himsel'. 'But when are they gaun to bury your mother?'

"'No till she dees, I hope,' says the lassie nebbily, for she thocht the man was joking. But it was owre late. Sandy was away wi' a cronie as drouthie as himsel', and didna come back till every groat o' the money was spent."

Thus proceeded this garrulous virago. Meantime John Coultar had left the quarries, and was on his way down the hill. He was jaded with work, and hungry. Why was not his wife waiting for him at the door as usual? He was dispirited and out of sorts, as he sometimes was, without being able to tell the reason why. He tried, however, to drive off worry and fatigue by the thought of the heartsome meal and the cheery smile awaiting him, and so he hastened down the hill to his own door.

CHAPTER XVI.

THE MINISTER'S RECORD (*continued*).

SINCE the birth of my third bairn, it has been borne in on my mind that my own stipend and my wife's small income do not so far overlap my temporal wants as they were wont to do. Somehow, under the stern but economical reign of Mrs. Pyat, the overlap from my stipend alone formerly amounted to a good wheen pounds of sterling money in the year, so much so, indeed, that I was able to begin my wedded life, after all expenses had been paid, with a small balance in the bank; but year by year the sum at my credit has grown sensibly less, which leads me to opine that I must either get my income augmented or take a "stave out of my cog," as the saying is. The circumstances that led me into this train of reflection occurred in this wise. An unexpected and great honour was, I may say, thrust upon me; for it was in no sense of my own seeking. The Earl of Killie, under whose patronage I hold the spiritual charge of the parish, with the manse, glebe lands, and other temporalities effeiring thereto, complimented me with a special invite, delivered by the hand of his own serving-man, to dine with his Lordship at the castle. This unlooked-for condescension put me in a sore flurry, insomuch that the pen trembled with agitation as I sat down to indite an answer, the which I was requested to do by the hand of the flunkey-lad who had brought his Lordship's letter. After I had despatched it, I was troubled with serious misgivings that the literary quality of the missive was not all it should be; for I have found that my greatest literary successes have always been achieved in the seclusion of my own room, when there was no one by to disturb the equanimity of my mind. But much greater concern laid hold on me by and by when my wife, who had been turning out the chest of drawers in which my dress things were kept, came into my study with the coat in her hand, the back and oxters of which were so riddled with moth-bites that, when I put it on, it parted in several places at once. My wife being brought up to the use of wardrobes and open presses for clothes, never, it seems, jaloused there was any danger to them in a close chest; and though, by my advice, she afterwards sent down to Matthew Spale's for cedar chips and shavings, which I had long known as excellent things for moths, this prudent action only applied to the future, and could in nowise repair the damage that had already been done. This was really a source of great distress to me; for, while I was deeply obligated to Mr. Meldrum, the tailor in Ayr, for turning me out a new suit in an uncommonly short period of time, it carried off the last five-pound note of my early savings, and occasioned me deep concern, when I pondered on my growing responsibilities, when there was so little prospect of augmented means.

The party at Lord Killie's was unquestionably a grand affair. It happened during the recess in the Parliamentary session, and the company, with the exception of some well-off county magnates and myself, was composed of Tory members of Parliament. To me was intrusted the care of a worthy dowager lady, who, albeit she had the air and breeding of a great family, joked with me real cantily because I offered her the wrong arm in taking her in to dinner, saying that she generally found that literary people, and those who had to earn their living by the exercise of the brain, had sometimes difficulty in distinguishing between their right hand and their left. It was, in truth, a flattering and complimentary rebuke for my ignorance. I found her to be an excellent talker, well skilled in compliment, and fairly conversant with the great subjects that were at the moment agitating the political and religious world. When the ladies had retired to the withdrawing-room, the bottles were pushed round, and the conversation became most interesting. After discussing the probabilities of an early overthrow of Lord Melbourne's Government, with the consequent accession of the Tories to power under Sir Robert Peel, Lord Killie skilfully guided the discussion round to the point which was to me of much more serious import, namely, the contention then going on between the ecclesiastical and civil courts, the which Lord Aberdeen's Act had just been introduced to bring to an end. It was a great privilege to hear these men, high in place and power, conversing quite frankly and with great understanding on these important topics. I had just finished my third glass of sherry wine, and was settling down to the enjoyment of the intellectual part of the feast with a comfortable feeling of warmth all over my person, when I heard Lord Killie clearing his throat.

"We are mere theorists," I heard his Lordship say, "in these theological discussions, but we have one amongst us to-night whose knowledge of such matters entitles his opinion to respect, no matter to which side of the controversy he may lean." All eyes were now turned on me. It was a trying ordeal, for which I was but ill-prepared. But through the Divine blessing I was for the occasion gifted with wonderful readiness of speech, and notwithstanding of the high personages by which I was surrounded, when I got to my feet my mind was preserved in perfect calmness.

"My Lord," said I, "since your Lordship has

been so good as to call upon me for an expression of opinion regarding the great and momentous question now stirring the country, it behoves me to do so with great humility in the presence of such a noble and influential assemblage. My Lord, I cannot help thinking we are going grievously astray in giving so much power, both political and ecclesiastical, to an ignorant, and, I may be pardoned for adding, self-willed people. The Whigs in the State, and the Evangelicals in the Church, are responsible for having scattered these seeds of what they call liberty, and which are now growing up everywhere around us, bearing fruits of dangerous restlessness and discontent. My Lord, it is the tendency of ignorance to be suspicious, and of ignorant people to be jealous of those above them. Give ignorance power and it will assail without mercy those established institutions of our country that have been reared by its greatest minds, and approved by its highest intelligence. This ignorance will do, because it looks with suspicion upon what it cannot comprehend. Having got their Reform Bill with its extension of political power, they must needs have ecclesiastical changes too. The Evangelicals, following the example of the Whig Government, are not slow to foster and stimulate this cry for reform. They pass their Chapels Act, by the which a large accession is given to their voting power in the supreme councils of the Kirk. But before this they go clean contrar to the established **law** of the land, and by their Veto Act strike a fell blow at patronage, and placé the power of calling a minister practically in the hands of the people, allowing them to veto the nominee of the patron, without reason for their **so** doing being required at their hands. The Whigs have placed us at the mercy of mob law; and the Evangelical majority are not only playing into the hands of the people, **but** are setting them an example of lawlessness that **is** likely to lead to the gravest **issues.** They call **us** Moderates, my Lord, and truly I am not ashamed of the name. The other side has gone, not only beyond the bounds of moderation, **but, as has been** declared by our highest civil courts, they have actually broken **the** laws **of the** land. And, if in their immoderate **zeal** they **have** gone owre far to turn back without the loss of their meagre store of self-respect, let them **leave us** in the peaceful enjoyment **of** our constitutional rights. Let them give up their state benefactions and temporalities, and cast in their lot with that radical and free people whose spiritual rights they have been so forward to champion and conserve."

My spirit was moved within me, and the growing sympathy which I could plainly discern in the faces of the exalted personages near by, carried me further, and caused me to use words of greater warmth than had been my **intention** to **employ**; nevertheless, I could clearly perceive the remarks were not ill-pleasing to my noble patron, who sat the while, smiling, and aye bow-bowing his head with kindly approval, as I went on. One thing I must not fail to note. While I found my way to the castle by the aid of Her Gracious Majesty's post-cart, his Lordship ordered his own carriage to be put in readiness to take me home, at which, when I arrived, there was no small rejoicing and glee, for my own and my wife's heart was greatly uplifted by the thought of receiving so much consideration at his Lordship's hands; nor was this consideration shown to myself alone, for, ere yet the carriage had departed from the castle-door, the butler had placed in my hands a sonsy package, the which, when opened, bred much daffing and hand-clapping among the bairns, for it contained great wealth of comfits and bonbons, that kept them in remembrance of my visit to the castle for many days. I have often been led to think, however, that as the web of the weaver has bars of black weft woven side by side with bars of a light, or, I may say, gayer colour, so the web of our experience has oftentimes two or three shots of gey grim yarn thrown in unaccountably amongst the brighter texture of our joys. The ways of Providence are truly inscrutable. It is a true word which says that the deep things of life are concealed from the wise and prudent, while they are often revealed to babes. I am moved when I think of the mysterious forecasts of fortune uttered by that strange spae-woman, Mysie Shaw, for, true enough, when she uttered the demented cry, and disappeared among the whins, her poor bairn was lying drowned at the bottom of the burn. The awsome, wandering creature, it seems, had been scrambling among the rocks near the place where the water tumbles over the linn, and I do not mislippen but he lost his grip, and would be mortally injured by the fall. At all events, there were nine several bruises on his person, and he was found some distance below, in that part of the water adjoining William Dickie's meadow, known as the Carlin's Pool. Poor Mysie! I am told she is to be seen night and day wandering about the banks, where the odd creature, her son, used to spend so much time, which, at best, must be but poor comfort. This calamity is not without admonishment to myself. What her remarks about my own personal trouble may mean I cannot tell, but the thing often pricks my heart with pain when I think on the part of her prediction that referred to herself having such speedy fulfilment. I am daily witnessing a growing unsettlement in the minds of my people, and if dissatisfaction with my own ministry is what the spae-woman's remarks about myself pointed to, the thing is actually coming to pass.

The chapel-minister of Beith—he has now been admitted by the late Act to rule as well as to preach —has been over here again, without my sanction, trying to stir up dispeace on the subject of the Veto Act, as illustrated by the disputed settlement of Mr. Edwards in the parish of Strathbogie. The meeting was held in Matthew Spale's cart-shed, and, as it was attended by a goodly number of my own kirk-members, I was stirred up on the following Sabbath-day to preach a sermon, as I thought, fitted to the occasion. I had given the matter serious, or indeed, I may say, profound meditation. My text was taken from Zechariah xi. and 2d—"Howl, fir tree, for the cedar is fallen." I presumed that the people had gotten their way; that ignorance and presumption had laid the axe at the root of the great cedar, the State Kirk, and that the whole fabric had tumbled to the ground. I was careful to depict in touching language the sacred growth of the venerable tree; the struggles through which it had passed; the precious blood that had been spilled by our noble ancestors to preserve it from skaith and harm; and then I drew a picture of the glorious fruits it had borne during all the long years it had flourished in the land. Now, what had the Vandals to put in its place? The land was to be planted with a set of lank and hungry fir-trees, from which neither fruit nor shelter could be expected. What could it be but a weary battle for existence, each one trying to swell its own rind, and fatten at the expense of its neighbour? Nay, was it not pitiful to look at this sorry picture? Surely the cry of the text was the only one that fitted the occasion, the only one that was patriotically and morally appropriate—" Howl, fir tree, for the cedar has fallen."

But no, I said, banish this miserable dream. It is, thank God, only an horrible nightmare, from which we are thankful to shake ourselves free. The grand old cedar has not fallen. The Lord of the Vineyard has not allowed its enemies to cut it down. It is the duty and privilege of the State, of this parish, and of every individual connected with it, to stand by the venerable tree, not only to guard it from ruthless hands, but to tend and nurture it, so that, in the words of the Psalmist, it may be like a tree planted by the rivers of water, that bringeth forth his fruit in his season. I was marvellously aided by Divine help in the preparation of this discourse, and had unwonted freedom in its delivery. My wife told me afterwards I was just like one out of the body, which is not to be wondered at when I think of the state of mind I was in at the time. She confided to me that in one passage I spoke with such unction that the dear wee bairns started to their feet, and contemplated me with alarm pictured on their earnest and innocent faces; and that at another time my own servant-woman was found, as she eloquently expressed it, with her faced bathed in tears. Truly the wind bloweth where it listeth, and it is whiles hard to tell whence it cometh or whither it goeth! These incidents may appear as trifles to some, but they are trifles that show the direction of the wind during the period to which this simple record refers. There is a single incident more to relate. Lord Killie did me the honour to call at the manse before departing to resume his Parliamentary duties, and informed me that the few remarks I had made at the castle on the political and ecclesiastical situation were well timed, and had done me no harm. It was truly a kind and generous thing of his Lordship to do, and is set down here more to illustrate his Lordship's considerate courtesy of manner than with the view of sounding forth my own fame.

PART FIFTH

CHAPTER XVII.

A MISUNDERSTANDING.

The first break in the even current of John Coultar's wedded bliss had taken place. The unwelcome neighbour had beaten a hasty retreat and left husband and wife face to face with the shadow of a broken confidence between them. What was the young wife to do? Her first impulse (generally the best in such dilemmas) was to run and throw herself into his arms, tell him how it had all come about and acknowledge the indiscretion; but John's look was stern and forbidding. There was no explanation invited. He had been deceived, his wishes had been ignored, and that was sufficient. He went over to the table, picked up the small empty bottle and smashed it to atoms behind the fire.

"So it has come to this," he said, in cold, biting tones. "Friendliness of this nature couldna have been cemented in a single day. Your husband's companionship wasna enough for ye, and a' my advice and anxiety for your sake has been in vain. But it was just what I feared." He sat down in the arm-chair with a dejected look, and gazed into the fire. There was a strange yearning in his heart towards his wife under all this severity of words. He would fain have taken her in his arms and kissed away that frightened, guilty look, but she had acted very unwisely, and, would it not be better, in fact he believed it would be the truest kindness in the end, to make an impression now? He *had* made an impression, but it was not what he intended. He did not know how keenly every word he uttered had bitten into her soul.

"I suppose you have nothing to say for yoursel'," he remarked by and by.

"Yes," she replied, "I had something to say a wee while since, but your words have cut it out o' my heart—I canna say 't noo."

They sat down to supper in silence. Next morning they separated for the first time without the customary kiss. John wondered all day if she would come out to meet him as usual in the evening. Even that, he thought, would show her regret for what had taken place. It would at least open up a way for talking the matter quietly over. When she had the supper spread she went to the door. Yes, he was coming down the hill. It was his place, however, to speak the first word of reconciliation now. He might surely do that, she thought, after the cruel way in which he had already spoken. She went inside and waited. He came in, and when she dared to look in his face, her heart sank within her. There was still the same dignified, stern expression there. They were both disappointed.

On the morning of the third day, he rose as the first gleams of light entered their dwelling. Marion was not asleep—indeed she had slept but little since that spirit of evil had brought disunion into their home. There was something unusual in his manner to-day; she saw that. He went about the house gathering up, and packing past, certain articles in a small travelling-bag. She too, rose and put on her things. Surely he would not break her heart by going away. Surely this was too great a punishment for the trifling, but unintentional slip of which she had been guilty.

"John," she said, driven to despair at last, "what does all this mean?"

"Mean," he retorted with calm severity; "it is for you to make out what it means. You have had three days and three nights to think about your folly, yet it never seems to occur to ye that you have done anything amiss." Had he stopped here, in spite of the severity of his tone, and the continued exaggeration of her offence, she would have been at his feet in a moment, but he proceeded—"I was anxious that ye should choose your company, that you should either keep yoursel' to yoursel' a'thegither, or if you did seek company among your own sex, that it should be such as would teach ye no ill. Instead o' that you have sought out, or, at all events, you have taken into your confidence, one who, from what I saw, has been suffered without rebuke to give ye a lesson in habits that are fitted to make us baith a byword in the place—yet ye have done no ill—no, no, there is nothing to be sorry for, and nothing to confess."

Marion, who had commenced to prepare her husband's breakfast, was stung and silenced by the injustice of his remarks. She had been on the point of asking his forgiveness; of explaining what a simple and accidental thing it was that had taken place, but how could she do that now? His confidence was broken; his love was turned into bitterness. She sat down in a chair, mentally crushed, and not daring to look at the stern and apparently loveless face. She was degraded in her own eyes. Her heart was stricken, and the pang was too deep for tears. John waited a moment, but there was no response. Had she but looked up pleadingly, had she wept or given any token that this lesson which he had endeavoured so dramatically to enforce, had produced the effect intended, he was ready to forgive all, but she gave no sign.

"Well, I am going," he said, turning away. "Sin without repentance is a hopeless thing. I canna tell ye when I may come back. I am ordered to the other quarries, where things have gone wrong; but you will find as much siller in the chest as will serve your turn in the meantime." Was it possible, she thought, they were to part without a reconciliation? Was there not time for that even yet? Marion rose—

"Ye will take breakfast before you gang, surely?"

"No," he replied, taking the travelling-bag in his hand. "I have stayed owre lang already. Maybe you will think the matter over when I am away, and if it chances to cross your mind that you have anything to say, you can write." John went out into the cool morning air with a heavy heart. He joined the post-coach at the crossing of the roads, and about mid-day was set down at the village of Auchincorby, within half a mile of the quarries to which he had referred. The Glenbuckie and Auchincorby quarries belonged to the same owner. John had heard for some time that things were not going well at the latter; but a crowning misfortune had occurred—the water of an adjoining mill-lade had found its way in some mysterious manner into the most profitable part of the workings, and now, plant, stock, and working utensils were some five feet under water. John Coultar immediately set to work. First of all, he detected and repaired the defect in the lade, thereby stopping the inflow of the water. Then came the question of emptying the quarry. The appliances at his disposal, such as pumps, etc., were of the crudest description, and after several days and nights of almost incessant labour very little progress had been made. During all this time the manager had been in the forefront, directing, encouraging, and often doing the labour of two men with his own hands. This activity left him very little time to brood over his domestic trouble. He was, however, in daily expectation of that letter which he hoped would put everything straight again. After that they would understand each other better; and he, for his part, would do his utmost to save his wife from similar vexations in the future. A week passed, but no letter came.

It had rained heavily for a couple of days, and, to add to the dilemma, several of their pumps had given way. It was miserably slow work. In the midst of these misfortunes, and suggested by them, an idea occurred to him, which, after consultation with the resident foreman, he resolved to carry out. This was to drain the quarry into Auchincorby burn, the channel of which lay about 100 feet below them in a rocky ravine. John at once drew his men off from the pumps, and employed them in cutting a channel for the water towards the burn. This done, he commenced the more delicate operation of piercing the quarry itself. This was effected by cutting and blasting, and in the course of a couple of days they had penetrated to within three feet of the water. Great caution was now observed. Two men, secured with ropes in case of accident, prepared what was considered to be the final charge, the fuse was attached and lighted, and they all retired to a safe distance to watch the result of the blast. It went off, but the water failed to come. The men still held back, but John Coultar ran down the slope and stepped into the cutting. He had been several minutes out of sight, when they heard repeated sounds as if the manager were testing the face of the rocky wall with a hammer. This was followed by a report, as if another charge had been fired, and in an instant the flinty barrier gave way, and the brown water, surging with terrific force through the opening, hissed and foamed down the face of the hill towards the ravine. . . .

Meantime Mrs. Coultar endured meekly her solitary penance at home. The memory of her husband's stern face and bitter words haunted her day and night. She knew, however, he would not be permanently unjust. Maybe his work had fashed him; indeed, she knew that the thought of Auchincorby quarry not getting on had given him much concern. Then he had to speak so sharp to the men at times that he had maybe got into the habit of saying things severely when he was angry. She knew he was quick-tempered, but it was often just a flash and by. She had faith that when he had time to think over all that had taken place he would write her a line generously admitting that he had treated her badly. At any rate, for herself, she resolved it should be a lesson to her for the time to come. Having arrived at this point, she took out her spinning-wheel, and setting it in the kitchen, commenced to card some wool which her grandmother had sent from the farm. No one should ever know they had quarrelled—no, not even her grandmother. It was so foolish of them both, but no one, so far as she was concerned, would have occasion to cast it up to them. The young wife worked hard for several days converting her wool into yarn. She would show John how diligent she had been. He would see for himself when he returned that she was not so fond of company as he supposed. Having brought herself to this frame of mind, Mrs. Coultar began to realise how difficult it might be for her husband to get time to write. She had heard of the flooding of the quarry, and learned that John was working himself off his feet. He had said on going away if she had anything to say she might write. That was a gey cutting remark; but he was going away at the time without his breakfast, and that maybe made him say sharper things than he meant. Her grandmother had told her before they were married that if ever they had words it was her place to give in first. Well, she would act on that good advice. What had she to live for now but him? She got to her feet, put past her work, and brought out materials to write. As she did so a heavy foot was heard approaching the door in haste. Her breath came and went quickly. Perhaps it was he. The door opened—no, it was only the resident foreman from Auchincorby. He was flushed and out of breath. Mrs. Coultar saw there was something wrong as the man took off his cap and stood to recover breath and composure.

"There is something the matter," she cried. "Dinna hide it from me. Is John ill?"

"Yes," he replied, "he's ill; he's got himsel' hurt at the quarry, but—but ye maunna gie way and faint, or the like o' that, for they're just coming up the hill wi' him, and will need ye to gie us a' the help ye can."

* * * * *

It was some time before John Coultar recovered consciousness, and several days elapsed before he was able fully to realise what had taken place. He had had a marvellous escape. When the pressure of water abated sufficiently to enable the men to institute a search for him, they found his body covered with loose stones and soil, firmly wedged in at the back of a boulder near the base of the hill. This had saved him from being carried into the rocky bed of the ravine. He had received a severe cut on the back of the head, and though none of his limbs were broken, which was a marvel, he had been terribly shaken. For some days the manager's life hung in the balance, but his wife laboured with heroic courage and tenderness. Night and day she watched over him till the critical moment had passed, and he was pronounced on the fair way to convalescence. As yet they had spoken but little to each other. Indeed, much speaking on either side had been strictly forbidden by the doctor. So far as John was concerned, it was not necessary to speak, for all his wants were most considerately anticipated. The doctor, however, could not hinder him watching and thinking. One day, after a long while's exercise of this kind, he took his wife's hand and held it for some time without speaking. Her eyes were averted, for they were full of tears; but they were tears of thankfulness and joy.

"Marion," he said, "you are a brave lass. Will you give me a kiss?" Marion did as she was requested to do, and afterwards hid her face in the coverlet.

"Dinna be ashamed, my dear," he said tenderly. ("Dear" was a word he seldom used, and to his wife's ear it had a significant sweetness.) "It has been very silly of us both, this quarrel; and I have been far sillier than you."

"Now," she interrupted, looking at him with a bright gleam in her wet eyes, "dinna say another word. The doctor says you're no to speak."

"Oh, I'm stronger than the doctor thinks. I believe I could get up this minute; but I'll maybe no do that for a day or two yet. I have been lying here thinking that spae-Mysie's prophecy wasna that far wrong."

"Yes," she said quickly, "a' through your illness I was thinking o't. She said the dead-claes wouldna be needed for a guid while to come. There was comfort in that. It was a sore trial; but I kent fine ye would get better."

Mrs. Coultar ran off with a buoyant foot and brought a small basket of woollen yarn to the bedside. "See that," she said, "I wasna idle. I havena seen a neighbour since ye gaed awa'. I wasna even at grandmother's. I was busy spinning a' the time, so that nobody kens. Now," she continued, "ye maunna say a single word more. I was a' to blame from the first, for I didna see things then as I do now; but just you lie still and get better, for I have a heap o' things to say by and by when you're stronger, that I daurna tell ye now."

CHAPTER XVIII.

POLEMICAL.

Whatever might be said about their attention to the common concerns and duties of life, no one could fairly charge the parishioners of Glenbuckie with lack of zeal in matters ecclesiastical. The agents of Intrusion and Non-intrusion had done their best to enlighten Glenbuckie, as well as other parishes in Scotland, on these all-absorbing questions; while the people themselves, with characteristic relish for such matters, were not slow to take up the arguments which fell from the lips of their instructors, and apply them after their own fashion.

To those not conversant with the constitution and practice of the Established Kirk of Scotland of that period, it may be necessary to explain that when a parish became vacant by the death, resignation, or deposition of its minister, it devolved on the patron to nominate a qualified person to fill the vacancy. In the document of presentation the patron directs the Presbytery " to take trial of the qualifications, literature, good life, and conversation" of the presentee, and of his fitness "for the functions of the ministry at the church to which he is presented." After the people had an opportunity of hearing his "trial sermon," or sermons, as the case might be, they were requested to signify whether they were prepared to give him "a call" to be their minister. For some time prior to the period of which these Chronicles treat, the call of the people had been practically set aside; for though it was still retained as a matter of form, it frequently bore only a few signatures, and these not always of persons who were members of the vacant church. On this nominal representation calls were sometimes given, and vacant charges filled. While patronage, as a rule, was distasteful to the Scottish people, it could be borne, so long as the patron was careful to select men who were calculated to command respect. Unfortunately, however, this was not always observed; indeed, patronage was too often looked upon by the person exercising it, more as a means of providing a comfortable place for a friend or favourite, than as implying the duty of supplying the people with a suitable spiritual guide and pattern. It is not surprising, therefore, that settlements made in these circumstances were looked upon and resisted as intrusions on the religious liberties of the people; and it was not uncommon to find armed representatives of the civil power called in to protect presbyteries in tying the outward knot on that spiritual cord which is supposed to bind pastor and people together.

The Church was composed of two sections known as Evangelicals and Moderates, resembling in some sense the Whig and Tory elements in the State. The former were the party of progress, whose battle-cry for the time was Non-intrusion and Spiritual Independence. The latter were really what their name implies. They were the comfort-loving, easy-minded class, who were opposed to change either in doctrine or Church government. Many of them were excellent and God-fearing men, who apprehended great danger to the Church from the views entertained by the earnest but restless spirits on the Non-intrusion side; and indeed it may be said that it was only in their opposition to the Evangelical proposals that they belied their name.

The passing of the Chapels Act by the General Assembly of 1834 resulted in the Evangelicals becoming the dominant party in the Church Courts. In the same year what is known as the Veto Act was carried through the House by the same party. By the latter Act the dissent of a majority of any congregation against a presentee practically abolished patronage, at least in so far as the patron's power to overrule the majority was concerned. Numerous appeals to the civil courts followed the passing of this Act. On the one hand it was held to be an offence of the gravest kind, and punishable by expulsion from his office, for a minister of the Church to invoke the civil power against any sentence passed on him by his ecclesiastical superiors. On the other hand it was maintained that the **Veto Act** affected civil rights; that in fact it was a violation of the **Act** of Queen Anne, and that it was *ultra vires* of the General Assembly to pass such an enactment. As is well known the appeals to the Court of Session resulted in interdicts, which, in turn, led to forced settlements, and scenes of an unseemly, and, in some cases, of a scandalous character. The House of Lords, however, supported the decisions of the inferior Courts; and as the legislature failed to step in to part the civil and ecclesiastical combatants, the Evangelical clergy in the month of May **1843**, casting aside State bonds and State emoluments, marched out from the floor of the Established Assembly Hall, and set up the Free Church of Scotland.

As was natural, the parishioners of Glenbuckie, like others, were much exercised by the questions which for the moment were moving the whole land. Janet Pyat, who was perhaps the most uncompromising Evangelical in the parish, had **once** more turned her back on the minister's family in spite of the witchery of the twins. The minister's views, she believed, were becoming more and more Erastian. This spiritual deterioration, she observed, had begun with his marriage. How could it be otherwise?

English boarding-school religion was "poor fushionless stuff, with neither beginning nor end, back nor middle." When the great day of decision should come, what could this timid worldly girl do but advise her husband to relinquish his spiritual independence, and cling to the loaves and fishes? These were some of Janet's musings prior to the final breaking of the tie which bound her to the family. She laid most of the blame of her master's spiritual backsliding at Mrs. M'Whinnie's door. The conversations in the nursery lately had been mainly of a controversial character. Her mistress was rather sick of this ecclesiastical bickering, and would fain have had a more docile assistant at her side, for, as had been predicted, her hands were now so full of domestic concerns that she had little time for the consideration of matters beyond that sphere. Janet, however, had been serviceable to her on many important occasions. The minister himself could not overlook that. He had also great respect for her long and faithful service during the years of his bachelorhood. On these grounds her stern strictures on modern religious tendencies were tolerated by her mistress with exemplary patience. Janet had gone to hear Mr. Hyslop, the chapel minister from Beith, on Non-intrusion. Mr. M'Whinnie had refused the use of the church on the occasion, which was severely commented on; but Matha Spale had come to the front, and cleared his workshop for the meeting, in order that the parish might have further enlightenment on the great questions he had come amongst them to discuss. Mrs. Pyat went home from the meeting greatly oppressed in spirit. The Moderates had sold their birthright for a mess of pottage. The Ark of the Lord had once more passed into the camp of the Philistines. She had passed a sleepless night. Her temper, never sweet at the best, was less sweet on the following morning, when sitting in the nursery she reviewed the situation, as revealed by the chapel minister.

Mr. M'Whinnie was in the study, but his wife was accessible, so she resolved to have it out with her. Janet gave a few preliminary groans, indicative of a troubled spirit, whereupon the unsuspecting lady of the manse inquired the cause of her trouble.

"Trouble!" she repeated, casting her head in the air dangerously. "There is trouble everywhere. Your Civil Magistrate"—there was contempt in her look for all such dignitaries—"no content wi' the sword, has usurped the Power o' the Keys."

"What keys?" inquired her mistress innocently.

Janet stared at her for a moment with a look of pity. "The Keys o' the Kingdom o' Heaven," she replied. "Is it possible that you, Mrs. M'Whinnie, the wife o' a Presbyterian minister, doesna ken what's meant by the Power o' the Keys?"

"It may be my ignorance," said Mrs. M'Whinnie meekly, "but I have always understood that the

Lord and Head of the Kingdom alone could give admittance to it."

"True," admitted Janet, "true, in a sense; but what does the Confession say? It's a grand thing to have the Confession doctrine at the root o' your tongue. Here it is as I learned it at the feet o' the sainted Dr. Plunket: 'The Lord Jesus, as King and Head of his Church, hath therein appointed a government in the hand of Church officers, distinct from the Civil Magistrate. To these officers the Keys of the Kingdom of Heaven are committed, by virtue whereof they have power respectively to retain and remit sins, to shut that Kingdom against the impenitent, both by the Word and censures; and to open it unto penitent sinners, by the ministry of the Gospel, and by absolution from censures, as occasion shall require.' Yet what will your civil powers do, but rampage into the sacred precincts o' the Kirk, like very bulls o' Bashan, and trample this grand doctrine under foot? See their ongauns at Lethendy, where a whole presbytery o' righteous men are dragged before the Court o' Session for no other offence than placing in the vineyard a labourer weel-tried and approven by a free and God-fearing people. See this Erastian presbytery of Strathbogie, what they will do. I am tauld they have inducted a graceless man—a wolf in sheep's clothing—into the parish o' Marnock against the solemn protest of 3000 souls, on the ground that ane Peter

Taylor, the keeper o' a change-hoose, had signed the call. But that's no the hauf o't. No wonder the reverend and godly Mr. Hyslop nearly broke doon in the middle o' his discourse, when telling o' these graceless cantrips; no wonder he had to rest on the bench and ask Matha Spale to fetch him a drink o' water before he could proceed. Oh, it's grievous to think o't. It seems the Courts o' Parliament are no ae bit better than the Lords o' Session. They are a' buckled wi' ae hasp. They are a' the ministers o' Satan, and how the Lord can restrain Himsel' from raining doon a fiery judgment on them beats me to see; for since the days o' Prelacy no Civil Magistrate, as I have been tauld, has ever dared to usurp the Power o' the Keys."

Mrs. M'Whinnie, although a Presbyterian minister's wife, had never read the Confession of Faith. The book, it is true, had been recommended to her by her husband as an excellent summary of doctrinal truth, but ere she had time to open its pages the cares and embarrassments of dual children fell to her hand. She was innocently interested, however, in the passage which Janet Pyat had just recited to her, and Mrs. M'Whinnie owned the unprudential habit, when things were not quite to her mind, of plainly saying so, regardless of consequences. In less honest, or at least in more politic hands, the rupture which ensued might have been avoided.

"About this Power of the Keys," she said, looking

up from her knitting thoughtfully, when Janet had talked herself out of breath. "I am not quite sure that I caught your meaning, Mrs. Pyat."

"Weel?" interrogated the person addressed, looking over her specs.

At the moment Mrs. M'Whinnie was passing the Glenbuckie session under mental review, and recalling some traits in their character which had come under her own observation during her sojourn amongst them.

"Well," she said, after this hurried survey of the local custodians of the Keys, "am I to understand the Confession doctrine says that the Keys of Heaven are committed to kirk-sessions, and that they—the kirk-sessions—have power to retain and remit sins as they feel disposed; and that further they have power to shut the Kingdom against what they consider the impenitent, and open it to those they think penitent?"

"That is the truth as formulated in the Westminster Standards," admitted the ancient Gamaliel.

"Then, Mrs. Pyat, it's a wicked, popish doctrine, and I for one don't believe it!"

Janet jumped to her feet with a bound. The earth seemed to tremble under her, and for the moment she felt like one who had received a treacherous blow. On recovery she hurriedly left the room, and returned wearing her bonnet and shawl, and carrying a small box in her hand.

"I have borne much wi' ye," she said, with an effort at judicial calmness. "I have tholed a deal for the sake o' thae puir innocent weans, but endurance has come to an end. Ye have never been stablished, strengthened, or settled, but I didna look on ye before as beyond hope. I now shake the dust off my feet as a testimony against ye, and I can only pray the Lord, whose word ye deny, that He may have mercy on ye before it's too late."

CHAPTER XIX.

RICHIE NEEBIKIN'S COURTSHIP.

SPAE-MYSIE'S remark that Jeanie Borland had a "licht heart and licht ways" did not lessen Richie Neebikin's regard for her. While Jeanie was admittedly "fond o' fun," Richie was no less soundly in earnest. His material prospects were not over bright. Yet he had a glimmering hope that if Jeanie would have him they might get the bowing[1] of some small farm, where she would be of infinite service to him in the management of the cattle. Richie was as yet very uncertain of his footing. A love-suit could not be pressed without words, and while his feelings, in a way, were strong enough, he was but an indifferent hand at expressing them in such a manner as was likely to captivate

---

[1] That is, to take a farm in grass with the live stock on it. This is a common practice in Scotland. When a farmer has more land and more stock than he can personally superintend, he hands it over to some person to manage, receiving such percentage as may be arranged. The farm and stock still remain his property. The person who takes the management is called a *bower*.

the affections of this rollicking and light-hearted girl.

William Dickie had gone to Matha Spale's to inquire into a report which was said to be in the newspapers, to the effect that the Duke of Argyll had passed a Bill through Parliament for the purpose of legalising the Veto Act, and Richie, feeling the restraint of an over-vigilant supervision removed, laid down his flail, went to the barn-door, the upper part of which was open, and laying his arms on the under half, looked out into the morning sunshine and commenced to hum, dreamily, a favourite ditty:—

> "Oh, sowens is a sliddery meat,
> And kail's a blash o' bree;
> But porridge is the life o' man,
> And brose is clag 'im tae."

There was a fine scent of new beans in the air. It was just after breakfast-time, and the poultry, having finished the repast which Mattie, the maid-of-all-work, had laid down for them, were stepping about the barn-yard in the gayest of spirits. The cock, who had upset the cog in which the morning meal had been served, mounted the small elevation thus afforded him, and gave a lusty crow in defiance of intrusion, and looked about him with his head now on this side and now on that, in a self-satisfied and masterful way; while the hens, like fine ladies taking a dirty crossing, stepped about in a dainty, coquettish fashion, jerking and casting their thoughtless heads, and singing the while their three or four notes of a song, as free of concern as if the Corn-Laws had been abolished, and as if that self-conceited polygamist on the cog had never given their gentle hearts a touch of pain.

> " Oh, sowens is a sliddery meat,
> And kail 's a blash o' bree— "

Richie opened the barn-door, and strode across the yard to the field beyond, whence he returned with half a sheaf of new-cut beans. These he commenced to "sheil" and eat with the view of supplementing an inadequate breakfast. The mistress, who had taken a "dwam" during the night, was unable to rise to superintend matters in the morning, and as she kept tight hold of the key of the "garnel," they had to patch up a meal of cold sowens with a farl of rye-bread thrown in to give it consistency. Richie revelled and ruminated over the beans till nature was comforted. Just where he stood, looking past the gable of the byre, he could see the bare bold crown of Goatfell glittering in the fresh sunlight; and lower down the shady side of the hill, thin dashes of blue smoke helped the imagination to realise that the white specks which glimmered amidst the green shadows on the shore were the houses of the Arran fisher-folk, who were doubtless at that moment drying and mending their nets on the beach. There was also visible between the two shores several miles of dazzling water, on which a ship, with white sails full-set, lay, as if at anchor, in the sunny calm. Richie's frame of mind, however, for the moment, was introspective—seascapes and landscapes, with ever so much picturesqueness, or with hills ever so high, were nothing to him.

> "But porridge is the life o' man,
> And brose is clag 'im tae."

He hummed this refrain quite mechanically, for just then even matters of diet could find no place in his cogitations. Some time before, Lammas fair had been celebrated in the county town. There he had forgathered with Jeanie Borland and her neighbour lass. At the same moment somebody else had forgathered with the neighbour lass, and, as they parted company, Richie, regardless of the expense, had taken his partner into a show. The marvels of the place were very absorbing, and the performance very short for the money, he thought; indeed, he was just beginning to realise and enjoy the thrilling novelties of the play, when the curtain fell, a great door opened, and he was thrust out again into a surging crowd, with the sweet responsibilities of a lass weighing heavily on his mind. As they walked along through the market-place, he felt as if he were drawing awkwardly in harness, and though he knew it was a harness which fitted him but indifferently, he would not willingly throw it off. After they had wandered about for some time in silence, he felt the duty of speech weighing painfully upon him, yet what was there to say ? At length he inquired—

"Did ye like the show, Jeanie ?"

The show for the moment had faded from Jeanie's memory under the excitement of newer sights and sounds, but she replied—

"Oh, it wasna bad."

After a while he resumed, as if the matter had been occupying his whole thoughts during the interval, "I'm glad ye liked it though, Jeanie. Would ye like to gang in again ?"

"What! Into the same show ?"

" Ay."

"Gae-wa, ye silly gowk, wha ever heard the like o' that ?"

Richie turned these reminiscences over in his mind in a phlegmatic, pleasant sort of way, as he gazed dreamily over the poultry-yard. It had not been a great beginning for him, he admitted. During their after perambulations through the fair, she had laughed at him, called him names, and afterwards he had lost her in the crowd. But Sandy M'Aull, the new cow-bailie, assured him at the time it was the way with most women, "for," said that authority, "the waur they misca' ye, and the mair they laugh at ye, the nearer they draw to ye in the end." Sandy was a roving blade, and being a favourite with the lasses made pretence of oracular knowledge of their ways. While Richie was taking what comfort he might from these reflections, somebody lifted the latch of the barn-door on the opposite side of that building. Richie at once knew the voice :—

> "Oh, she's a fickle, a fickle wild rose,
> A dam-ask, a cabbage, a chyn-ee rose."

It was the cow-bailie, who entered carrying a large basket of turnips.

"You're a gey boy," he said, "gaun on that gate doing nothing when the maister's awa.'" He laid down the basket, performed two or three steps of a hornpipe on the barn-floor, and resumed his song :—

> "We had groun up thegither like young apple-trees,
> We had clung to each ither like double sweet-peas;
> And now they have taken her to plant her in a pot,
> While I am left to wither all forsaken and forgot."

The hornpipe was again performed :—

> "Oh, she's a fickle, a fickle wild rose,
> A dam-ask, a cabbage, a chyn-ee rose."

"Man, Richie, ye sinner, I have news for ye. I have just seen that lass o' yours at the Mains. I telt her ye were going down to see her the nicht, and that I was going with ye as your black-fit."

"No——!"

"I did, though. I said ye were daft about her, and that I wasna muckle better about the ither woman, her neighbour. So ye have only to gang doon and hang up your hat." This blithe spirit whistled a merry stave, pitched his bonnet in the air, and pirouetted round the barn. At this point Mattie came in to inquire, on behalf of the mistress, what was the matter with Richie's flail, for though she (the mistress) "couldna see through the gavel o' a house," she was "geyan gleg at the hearing." Having satisfied himself by further investigation that the cow-bailie was not "sploring," Richie took up his flail, and sent the chaff and dust spinning to the rafters.

In the evening, after they had got the beasts foddered, and had taken their neep supper (the mistress declared they "should get no ither, for the wye they had idled their time when the maister's back was turned") they set off together for the Mains. The Mains got the credit of being what is called "a rough hoose," which meant, there was always plenty and to spare. On this occasion the master and mistress were from home, and in accordance with the hospitable traditions of the house, the lover and his black-foot were treated to a toothsome supper. Sandy M'Aull thereafter insisted on singing a comic song, in which there was some speaking, a dance round, and a shuffle in the middle, between every double stanza. This performance over, the black-foot retired with Jeanie's neighbour to the scullery, leaving the lovers to themselves.

"He's a gey lad that," said Richie, while the excitement of M'Aull's performance was yet upon him.

"Ay, he's a merry ane," coincided Jeanie, redding up.

"Oh, he's just a gey boy." The excitement had now somewhat cooled down, and Richie was beginning to realise the seriousness of being left to his own resources without a third party present to "push on the crack." After his last remark, which seemed to sum up in a laconic way all that he had to say about his brisk companion, he sat for some time in silence watching the young woman's movements. By and by, when she had things tidied up to her own satisfaction, she drew in a chair towards the fire and sat down.

"There's a guid seat here," Richie remarked, patting the wooden settle on which he himself sat. "I think this would haud twa."

"Oh, I can sit here fine. I'll get a better look at ye where I am."

Richie laughed with a heartiness out of all proportion to the humour of the remark. He, evidently feeling that he had done so, fell back for a space into a most melancholy silence.

"Ye have a mortal lot o' grand things in this hoose," he resumed, after a while, rubbing his chin, and gazing at the ceiling as if he could see them all there.

"Ay."

"Wonnerfu' fine chairs, and things."

"Oh ay."

"And—this settle—dod! I think it's aboot as prime a ane as ever I saw."

"Oh, it's a guid settle."

"Made by Matha Spale, I'll be bound." Jeanie could not vouch for the maker. She fancied it had been made before Matha Spale was born. Richie hitched himself to the other side of the seat, again stroked his chin, and gazed into the fire.

Meantime, M'Aull was apparently carrying the day in the scullery, to judge by the "daffing" that was going on there. Jeanie's inquiry as to what they were "up to ben there!" was answered by further laughter, evidently the result of brisk "toozling."

"He is a gey boy that," Richie re-affirmed, as if his first asseveration to that effect had been misunderstood. "Oh, he's an auld ane." In his heart of hearts he wished he could be a "gey boy" too. M'Aull had once told him that the only "wye to get on wi' women was to keep them lively." Richie thought seriously about this. He had a peculiar power of drawing forward his left ear by a slight movement of the muscles of his face. In his school-days this performance had been a source of great amazement and fun to the boys, who, with the aptness of characterisation common to school-days, had nicknamed him "Soople Lugs." John Humpleback, the late schoolmaster, had told him of a grand French lady—one Marie Louise, the second wife of the great Napoleon—who possessed a similar power, and who used to amuse the ladies of her court at their private soirees by turning her ears almost completely round. If this performance pleased grand French ladies, surely a simple country lass would derive some pleasure from it.

"Jeanie," he said, by and by, with much gravity, "would ye like to see me wagging my left lug?"

"Oh ye daft idiot," she screamed, almost falling off her chair with laughter. "Wha ever heard the like o' that?"

Richie leant forward that she might see there was no deception. Jeanie watched him for a second or two, and again burst into immoderate laughter.

"Don't do that, ye silly fule!"

"Oh, it doesna hurt me; see that, I can do it quite easy."

The merriment over this performance was so boisterous that M'Aull and the neighbour lass came into the kitchen to see what was the cause of it, and immediately caught the infection of laughter.

After this demonstration the evening passed briskly. Richie felt he had made an impression; and Jeanie put him quite at his ease by the glibness of her conversation. At last, when M'Aull got to his feet, and said they would need to be stepping—

"He'll step nane, yet awee," said Jeanie. "So ye

may just gang your wyes, and warm the bed for him, gin ye like." Jeanie pulled Richie by the sleeve as they escorted the cow-bailie to the kitchen door. When the latter had been dismissed she led Richie into the pantry, and inquired considerately for his mother. "Weel," she continued, "it was just this bit end o' a ham. I thocht maybe it would be tasty for her, if ye could rin hame wi't till her, without onybody kennin'." Richie could "do that brawly." After such touching and considerate kindness, what was to hinder him having a kiss, but Jeanie, declaring that ae thing was enough at a time, offered to let him out by the front door, in case that wild callant M'Aull should be waiting for him. Richie followed her through the dimly lighted lobby towards the door, when suddenly they were arrested by some one coughing on the stair.

"Mercy!" cried the deceiver, under her breath. "Has the maister come hame?"

"I didn't know I had visitors in my kitchen at this time of night," said the voice sternly. "Sir, may I make bold to ask who you are?"

Richie turned excitedly to face the figure on the landing, whirling the parcel he carried behind his back. "Me?" he stammered, "I'm a servant-man, sir."

"And may I ask what is your business in my house at this untimely hour, and what is that thing you are carrying so suspiciously behind you?"

"Oh—oh—behind me? Weel—it's—a fiddle, sir," replied Richie, terrified into the telling of an ingenious falsehood. The uncompromising figure on the stair laughed a low, hoarse laugh, in which Jeanie, who had retired to the kitchen door beside her neighbour lass, joined.

"Ah! a fiddle, is it? Well, I may say I am fond of music myself,—let us hear what you can do."

"But, sir, I havena a bow wi' me; I—I—never play without a bow."

"I'll soon get you a bow, my man," said the speaker, disappearing in the darkness, with rather a threatening tone of voice. "Hold on a minute, and I'll soon get you a bow."

Taking advantage of the disappearance of this unexpected and apparently dangerous questioner, Richie pitched the parcel gently towards the kitchen, and, opening the front door, took to his heels, and did not pause till he found himself safely in the loft above the barn, where he and the cow-bailie were wont to sleep. The latter had not yet arrived; indeed, at that moment he was dancing an Irish jig in the kitchen of the Mains while the two girls had fallen on the settle, perfectly exhausted with laughter at the "gey boy's" clever personation of the master. When M'Aull returned he expressed surprise at finding his bed-fellow home before him.

"I cam hame geyan hurriet," said Richie. "The maister cam in after you left, and fell foul o' Jeanie and me in the trance, as I was gaun out. It was an unlucky thing for her, but I took guid care the auld boy didna get my name."

"Lord, ay," said the hypocritical cow-bailie, "that was a guid thing, for if it had come to the maister's ears I'm thinking ye would have got laldie."

CHAPTER XX.

THE MINISTER'S RECORD (*continued*).

I HAVE been afflicted with a sad lowness of spirit since I penned my last record. The measles had entered our dwelling and were running their course among the dear bairns, when, to crown the dispensation, my servant-woman was laid low with the same tedious distemper. The only body that would approach my door was Peter Shule, the betheral, and though he could do but little to help us, it was a comfort to see even this frail representative of the outside world under my roof. I have not been in my own pulpit for weeks, for, as soon as the eruption made its appearance, and the thing got bruited abroad, I was waited on by three members of my session, who, it is true, expressed deep concern and sympathy for me, but suggested that I should provide for the maintenance of ordinances for some time to come, as if it should be known that I was to conduct the services while a smittle disease was raging in my house, the attendance at divine service would be sure to fall away, and the cause of religion might suffer great detriment thereby. I cannot say that I shared their fears of communicating the disease by appearing in the pulpit once a week, but to please them I gave way, and appointed a lad well spoken of by the Presbytery of Greenock, by name Ewan M'Quilkan, to fill my place. While the action of my session was doubtless prompted by the best motives, at the same time it humbled me sorely to think by what a slight tie our social relationships are bound together, and by what a simple dispensation Providence can make us feel as if we hadn't a true friend left to us in the world.

I went out the other day to take the air, for, between attending to the bairns and the servant-woman, my physical system was much in need of bracing, and while going along the highway I met several members of my own flock, who passed me by on the other side of the road. I may have been suffering from over-sensitiveness, but somehow I suspected that this distance, or as I may call it dryness, was not altogether due to the measles in my family, but that the differences of opinion which have recently sprung up amongst us on this Intrusion and Non-intrusion question had something to do with it. On these points, I admit, we are at variance, but that this should interfere with private friendships of so many years' standing produced in me exceeding heaviness of spirit. In the midst of this sore depression a wondrous thing happened. I was sitting in the study one day brooding over my troubles when Peter Shule, the betheral body, came in and told me that Major Macilorum was smitten with a grievous illness, and desired to see me. Now I looked upon this summons as a very strange thing, for this Major Macilorum, who lived in a lonely house situated half in Glenbuckie and half in a neighbouring parish, paid no heed whatever to the public ordinances of religion. Though it was well known he had no desire after such matters, he excused himself on the singular ground that he did not know to which parish he belonged, and being a man whose natural instincts inclined to war, he declared that if my reverend brother and myself would meet and do battle for him, he would go over to the first man that drew blood. I mention this pugilistic and ungodly remark, not from any levity of spirit, but to show the character of the man. For however anxious the ministerial shepherd might be to bring lost sheep into the fold, the method proposed by him for his own reclamation could have no other meaning than to bring ridicule and discredit on the calling, whose votaries have in all ages been recognised as the ambassadors of peace.

Anxious as I might be to obey the summons, and extend the consolations of religion to this poor sinner at the close of his worldly career, I felt it behoved me to warn him first of all that I had a smittle trouble in my own family, so that if he chose he might send for the Rev. Isaac M'Wheedle in the next parish; but when Peter Shule, the betheral, carried my message to him, it seems his wrath was kindled within him, and that in spite of his condition he indulged in very profane language, and inquired with asperity if I thought he was a child, and asked, with growing profanity, whether the fear of measles was likely to alarm a man who was already on the brink of the grave. When I went to see him he was truly in a dangerous case. His language to me was neither respectful nor complimentary, but I did not mind that, for he was suffering great pain. I offered up earnest supplication on his behalf, and as he was too weak to enter into conversation regarding his spiritual condition, I took my departure, promising to see him again on the following day. When I returned there was a marked change for the better in the condition of his health. There was a grim smile on his face as I took my stand by the bedside.

"When are M'Wheedle and you going to have that pitched battle?" he inquired. I answered him gravely, as became one speaking to a dying fellow-creature, that our warfare was a spiritual one, that our wrestling was with principalities and powers.

"Yes," he said, "that is with things no ordinary mortal can either see or get at. If you will wrestle, why not wrestle over poor devils like me? Why don't you carry the flesh and blood and brain of reasonable people along with you ? What profit is there in splitting hairs and lashing the wind ? Isn't it deplorable to see educated men wasting their lives in wordy controversy over mere fragments of fancied principle ? But it has been the way of the Church in all ages, and its leaders of the present day are no wiser than its leaders ever were. First you come to grief over the Marrow Controversy, then you divide and subdivide over the Burgess Oath, and now Patronage, the Power of the Keys, and God knows what else, is in everybody's mouth, and setting every man against his fellow. The ordinary concerns of life are going to the dogs. Ignorant men leave the plough rusting in the furrow to embitter their lives by quarrelling with each other about Non-intrusion and Spiritual Independence. What are your Secessions, your Burghers and Antiburghers, your New Lights, your Old Lights, and your United Secessions, unless they teach men to live peaceful and useful lives ?"

I was greatly taken aback by the tone and pith of the Major's remarks. I did not think that a man so completely beyond the pale of the visible Church could be in possession of such intimate knowledge of the harassments and disquietudes that prevailed within her borders. It was therefore with sorrow that I was constrained to admit that his observations were, alas ! too true.

"I should like to go to heaven myself," he continued, taking little or no notice of what I said; "but I hate your so called good people—that is, the good people I see around me—whose religion consists mainly of heartless formality and bigoted intolerance. I could not suffer to be everlastingly with them. But I like those who are straightforward, and considerate of others; just, honest, sympathetic, and self-denying people like what Jesus Christ and my own mother were—they made no parade of their goodness, but were willing, when need came, to lay down their lives for the sake of others: people who prefer doing a good turn to a neighbour, or an enemy for that matter, to singing psalms and making long empty prayers at street-corners. If heaven consists of a community such as one sees around him in the Church of the present day, then I pray that the Lord in His mercy may not take me there."

While I was greatly exercised in mind by this blunt and irreverent language, I could not but admire the earnestness of the Major's manner. The Spirit of the Lord was evidently stirring within him; but there was evidence of great chaotic darkness in his mind. As yet it was but the still, small voice crying in the wilderness; and as I went home, slowly and meditatively, through the quiet, green loanings, I offered up fervent supplication that the Spirit which moved on the face of the waters, and commanded light to shine out of darkness, might illumine his heart and mind, and lead him to a saving knowledge of the truth.

The dispensation which the Lord had sent upon me in the form of the measles having passed away without leaving even the dregs of harm behind them, I had gone through the usual course of burning that noxious-smelling thing brimstone in every room of the house, and was looking forward with thankfulness to the near prospect of being able to resume my duties, and of going out once more to mingle freely with the people. After consultation with my wife, I had caused Peter Shule to speak freely of the important fact that my dwelling had been disinfected, so that timorous friends might again rally around us, and strengthen our hearts with their sympathetic intercourse. William Dickie and Haplands were my first visitors. They came one evening at the gloaming, some days after the fumigation had taken place, and, as their manner seemed to be somewhat constrained, I took them into the study, and told them all danger of infection was now happily over.

William Dickie was the first to speak. He hoped that "our light afflictions, which are but for a moment, would work out for us a far more exceeding, even an eternal weight of glory." They had come, however, not to speak of bodily ails, but of a matter that had spread dismay and consternation over the parish, and which, as a session, he was afraid they could not overlook, and that was that my wife had declared she did not believe in the doctrinal standards of the Church. Haplands and he were fain to believe that such a charge might not be true; but they had it from a most trustworthy source, and they felt it incumbent upon them to inquire into the matter privately, if peradventure they might get the thing settled offhand, without breeding a scandal in the Parish. I need not say I was utterly astounded. That these uncouth, ignorant men should dream of attempting to subject my wife, who was at the time in a weakly and nervous condition, to private discipline, roused feelings in my breast which I could not well conceal. My first impulse was to show them to the door, and order them to look after their own affairs; but by a wonderful effort I was able to control my natural feelings. I answered discreetly, allowing that it was a most grave charge; but as I had never heard of such a thing, it was right and proper that they should name the trustworthy source from which the rumour took its rise. This, however, not being convenient, I was led to enlarge on the duty of truly Christian people endeavouring to protect each other from the calumnious misrepresentations which the enemies of the Lord, both inside and outside of the Church, were just then doing their best to heap upon the Lord's people. As for my wife, she had had but little time since coming amongst them to devote to the study of doctrinal questions, being much exercised in the upbringing of a small family; but it would be my duty to converse with her on the questions now raised, and explain what might require explication. Meanwhile, as a Church, they were passing through a season of great trial. It was the duty of every man to look well to himself and his own household; for whereas there ought to be only one path for all Christians, of late there had been divers ways opened up, and it behoved them all to be often on their knees, so that they might find, after the present strife and confusion was over, that they themselves had found entrance by the strait gate that leadeth unto life. I was moved to great earnestness of speech, for I could perceive there was a growing tendency abroad to magnify the letter to the detriment of the spirit of our sacred religion. Questions of mere Church-government, as Major Macilorum had truly said, were embittering the minds of the people, and usurping the place of essential Christian principles. When I afterwards mentioned the subject to my wife, and found out for the first time what had taken place between her and Janet Pyat, I was no longer in doubt as to who was at the bottom of this evil report. It grieved me exceedingly to think that one who had lived so long under our roof, and who had eaten bread at our table, should have lifted up the heel against us.

On the following Sabbath—being the first time

of entering the pulpit since the trouble in my family —I preached what I believe was a telling sermon. My text was taken from 2 Timothy iv. and 14th, "Alexander the coppersmith did me much harm: the Lord reward him according to his works." Janet Pyat was not present during the delivery of this discourse, having, as I learned, gone over to the sect called the Reformed Presbyterians; but I could perceive that that contrar woman Haplands slept less than usual that day, and as I urged home the lesson of my text in an application of great warmth, inveighing against the sin of taking up or circulating an evil report against a neighbour, I could see the woman was all mouth and ears with attention. This I was not sorry to observe, for of late Janet Pyat and she have been hand and glove, as the saying is, and I knew that the practical part of the discourse, at least, would be preached over again to the ancient dame; but whether for good or evil, the Lord alone can tell.

PART SIXTH

CHAPTER XXI.

THE PARISH TRIES TO MAKE UP ITS MIND.

The Moderate and Evangelical leaders had said their say. Arguments had been iterated and reiterated on both sides, and now it was felt the champions and their bewildered followers were nearing the valley of decision. Amongst the rank and file there might be some waverers, but the leaders were too deeply pledged to the cause they had espoused to desert; indeed they could not do so without facing the ruin of dishonour. It is but simple justice to say that stern principle, and not any consideration of worldly advancement or the reverse, was what actuated most of these reverend fathers and brethren in selecting their position in this great controversy, a controversy which was to rend asunder the solid ranks of the Kirk of Scotland. Those clergymen whose study of the great questions at issue led them to cling loyally to the Auld Kirk, could do so, not only on principle, but with the comforting knowledge that they remained with the loaves and fishes. The opposing majority, however, had no such consolation.

To renounce State control was to renounce State emoluments, house, home, and voluntarily to throw themselves into a new and uncertain sphere, in which they should have to bake their own bread and catch their own fish. In other words, they were called on to rise out of the lap of assured independence, leave all behind them and begin life afresh, putting their trust in God and in the sympathy and liberality of the people. Adherence to Evangelical principles therefore involved great self-sacrifice, and while the ministers would be the first to suffer, the burden of building churches, and providing for the maintenance of ordinances on the spiritually independent basis, would ultimately fall on the laity who adhered to them. These facts were clearly placed before the people. The course of events was fast hastening the controversy to an issue, and those who had not made up their minds felt that they must do so without delay. In Glenbuckie the large majority of church-goers had already declared for Non-intrusion. This result had not been arrived at without much serious questioning and consideration; and while the motives of a few might be open to suspicion, it must be added that the decisions of most were arrived at after a fairly intelligent view of the situation, and on grounds that were more or less honourable to themselves.

Two of the members of the Glenbuckie session had of late been much exercised as to which side they should take in the great spiritual contest: these were Haplands and William Dickie. They had numerous conversations over the matter, but Haplands could clearly see from recent hints thrown out in their discussions that William was gradually settling down on the Moderate side.

"It's a serious matter," said William Dickie one day as Haplands and he stepped along the loaning from church, with their wives following at a short distance. "A serious matter; for what says the Apostle? 'Put the people in mind,' says he to Titus, 'to be subject to principalities and powers, and to obey magistrates.'"

"And what, na, do ye think will be the meaning o' principalities and powers in that sense?"

"Just the rulers o' this world, the folk that mak' the law and rule."

"Weel, I would 'a thocht the passage had some high speritual meaning, such as gie'n in to the powers abune us; but then it says ye are to obey magistrates—surely the Scripture canna play fast and lowse, saying a thing in ae breath, and contradicting it i' the next. If ye are richt, dod! it mak's the wye a gey heap plainer for us."

"It's a solemn thing to break up a Kirk that is not only established by law, but by the blood o' Covenanters and martyrs."

"True, true," remarked Haplands; "so it is."

"Then," continued William, coming to the kernel

of the matter, "what for should we encourage a wheen ministers to run awa' from their present means o' living when the matter is so doubtful? Kirks maun be built, ye ken; and as for the ministers, the maist o' them in general have gey big families that maun be fed. Who is to do that, think ye?"

Haplands fixed his eyes on the cart-rut along the margin of which they were pacing, and shook his head gravely as much as to say, "Oh, just puir farmer bodies like you and me!"

"Then," proceeded William, feeling his question had at least been sympathetically answered, "if the Kirk wants purging, is it no the duty o' earnest men to stick by it till the old leaven is cast oot? The people need haudin' in by the head. They are far owre ready to run i' the direction o' every wind that blaws; and, as the minister says, it is the duty o' a' Christian governments to encourage and maintain the Protestant religion, while it is ours to stand by and see that the milk o' the Word is served out pure without money and without price, in order that the flock may grow up and be nurtured thereby."

Haplands was profoundly impressed by this view of the situation. He did not like to be disturbed by any sudden and violent change. Mentally he was too slow to adapt himself readily to new situations. The two men had now reached Haplands' gate, and they turned to see how their wives were getting up the hill. They were coming along, not far off, in that stiff, solid, unwieldy manner common to country matrons, who from lapse of time and other circumstances, have lost much of the grace of form and the poetry of motion which may have characterised them in earlier days. Looked at from the elevation to which their husbands had attained, a superficial observer acquainted with country ways might have supposed that they were—or at least Mrs. Haplands was—discussing a serious fall in the price of butter, or the disastrous congenital mortality which that year had been general over the parish amongst poultry. Haplands, however, knew better. He was an earnest student of his wife's face and manner. He had watched her carefully in church, and as he saw her then and now, he knew she was deeply stirred by ecclesiastical unrest. How he wished she could be induced to take William Dickie's sensible view of matters! As the women approached they slackened pace. As yet the crack had only reached the comma stage, so to speak; colons, semicolons, and other indications of involved speech had to be encompassed before the full period of the narrative could be reached. When this point had at length been gained, William Dickie saluted his neighbour's wife gravely, and inquired how she liked the solemn ordinances of the day.

"Ordinances!" she said contemptuously. "Is yon what ye ca' solemn ordinances? I wonder a wheen men-folk o' ye didna rise and leave the kirk.

Wha cares about Alexander the coppersmith ? But, in troth, it wasna Alexander the coppersmith ava' that did him the ill—it was puir, honest, downright Mrs. Pyat that telt an owre true tale about his ain wife. No, no, it'll no do, William. We maun get somebody into the parish who will preach us a gospel sermon, instead of raking up auld stories and flyting them out under the name o' Alexander the coppersmith." As she spoke she sidled through the gateway, while William Dickie and his partner, seeing from her heated manner that further conversation would not tend to edification, passed up the brae towards their own home.

Mrs. Haplands was not blessed with a sweet temper at any time, but it had been noted by her husband, after long and painful observation, that as soon as the Sunday gown went on her back, be it holy day or fair day, the mercury went down, and all in the house naturally prepared themselves to look out for squalls. This arose, not from depression in the surrounding atmosphere, but from the uncomfortable feeling in her own mind that she was under the tyrannical domination of good clothes. As they passed up the yard towards the door, Nanny, the servant-woman, who was sitting with her back to the kitchen window, reading Boston's "Crook in the Lot," came in for a share of her mistress's ill-humour.

"Now," she said, "just look at that. Was ever

onybody plagued like me wi' a heedless slype o' a woman?" Haplands knew without any verbal description the cause of the offence, and replied peaceably that it was "a gey ondecent-like thing."

"I should never leave my ain hoose," she continued, flinging the door back to the wall with a thud that made poor Nanny think of the "Crook in the Lot" as it affected herself. "What is the meaning o' having that blind rowed up to the tap o' the window on the Sabbath-day? Ye are auld enough to ken that sic a thing his never been allowed in my house. Dinna tell me it was owre dark to see the sma' print, ye back-spoken woman that ye are. What will the neighbours think o' a house that mak's no differs between common days o' the week and Sabbath-days? I wonner what ye were brought up to? It would be better for folk no to gang to the kirk ava' than to get angert this wye coming to a body's ain door." The mistress bounced ben the house in a bonny rage, while Nanny, who had drawn down the blind peacefully, proceeded to "dish the kail," remarking under her breath to the servant-man and the laddie who sat by the fire, that she wondered what guid her kirkin' did her, "coming hame ragin' that gate at the licht o' day."

After dinner the mistress sent the laddie, her son, "ben the house" to learn his "questions," and ordered Nanny to hearken him the two double verses of the Psalm she had told him to learn in the morning, so that when she (the mistress) came to hear him there might be no mistakes. Haplands moved uneasily in his seat, for he knew from the dismissal of the boy, and by the cast of his wife's countenance, that there was something on her mind.

"Weel," she said, speaking in a purposeful tone as the callant shut the door behind him, "what are ye for doing noo?"

"As regairds what?" her husband inquired innocently.

"As regairds what? As regairds the Kirk. Have ye made up your mind what ye are going to do? It's about time things had come to a settlement some wye, I'm thinking."

"Weel, what do ye say yoursel'?"

"Dinna throw the settlement on me," she retorted. "Ye are an elder o' the Kirk, and should ken what ye mean to do." The elder was turning over William Dickie's arguments in his mind while she spoke.

"Weel," said he, "it would be a gey spite to turn oor back on the Auld Kirk where the bluid o' the Covenanters and martyrs was shed; besides, it'll tak' a hantle o' siller to build new kirks, and sic like——"

"Weel?" she said.

"And I was thinking maybe we should just stick by it and purge oot the auld leaven, and—and mak' the best o' a bad bargain."

"And what about the Civil Magistrate?" she inquired.

"Weel, ye see the magistrates aboot these pairts are ceevil enough, and are no likely to gie us muckle fash, and if we could just manage to haud the people close by the head——"

"So ye mean to bide by the Moderates?" she remarked, anticipating what he was about to say.

"I was thinking that," he replied.

"Ay!" and she spoke sarcastically. "Weel, I wish them luck o' ye. As for me, I'll take my chance o' hearing sound preaching in Matha Spale's workshop."

"Hoot, toot, guidwife, we maunna be separated."

"But ye have your mind made up."

"Weel, my mind's no that sair made up; but William Dickie's biding wi' the Auld Kirk."

"And do ye think William Dickie's conscience is to rule the whole parish? No, no, guidman. Gang wi' William Dickie if ye like, but as for me and the callant, we'll never set foot in the Established Kirk again. I'm determined on that."

Haplands had thought his wife might be amenable to argument, but he felt he had somehow failed in bringing the matter home to her. He felt, also, it would never do for his wife and himself to attach themselves to two different Churches. Apart from the unseemliness of such a proceeding, he knew full well the domestic discomfort it would bring upon himself. It was, after all, he considered, very much a question of expense ; and if she could see her way to face the responsibilities of providing a new kirk for a new minister, he had better go peacefully along with her, for, as he said, after taking a fresh survey of the situation, "it is her I have to please, after a', and no William Dickie."

Matha Spale and Eneas M'Clymont had a keen search after the truth in another part of the parish. They had already gone over and cleared some polemical ground to their mutual satisfaction, but they came at last to a complete deadlock on the "Divine right of Conscience." The cartwright had hazarded a definition of this phrase, which led him into such an involved condition of mind, that at last, with the perspiration running down his face, he had to give it over with the admission that it was "a gey kittle thing to redd up."

"I suppose everybody has got a conscience," said the blanket-weaver, seeing his friend's confusion.

"I think we maun alloo that," Matha said. "We are told to hearken to the voice o' conscience. Now, if a man has no conscience, how can he hearken to it?"

"True, Matha. I believe everybody has a conscience o' one kind or anither; and if he gangs contrar to it, he is blamable, more or less." Thus qualified, Eneas felt he had overcome some preliminary difficulties, and established a fair case for argument.

"Weel?" queried the cartwright with a "fashed" look, for he was "clean sick" of these perplexing metaphysical subtleties.

"Weel!" continued Eneas, seeing the argument dimly before him, and hurrying on lest it should elude him, or get mixed up as his opponent's had done. "Suppose you have a conscience, and I have a conscience, do ye think it would be right for me to interfere wi' yours, or for you to interfere wi' mine?" The speaker looked as if he would like a simple yea or nay to this interrogation, inasmuch as if he answered it negatively he was prepared to proceed.

"No," said Matha decisively, "that would be wrang a'thegither, but the case o' the Kirk is waur than that. I may say you are wrang, or you may say I am wrang, and there the dispute between us ends; but the thing is different wi' Kirk and State. The State says to a parish, 'Here's a minister for ye, fresh from the hands o' the patron, take him in;' but after his 'trials' the parish says, 'No, we canna bide under this man's ministry. We dinna like his manner, his prayers, or his preaching.' Does this end the dispute, think ye? 'Oh no,' says the State, buckling on its swird, 'we canna alloo that. We are no to be thrawn wi' on ony sic grounds;' and so this power, wi' the swird at its back, comes doon wi' its dragoon sodgers, its civil magistrates, and ither armed forces, and claps the presentee into the minister's office against the **solemn** protest and dissent o' the people. Is there ony speritual independence there? Where **is** your **Divine** right o' Conscience in a case like that?"

M'Clymont felt as if his colloquist had fairly "coupet the harrows on him." What he had intended to bring **out** was that there should be more forbearance on **both sides.** It was admitted that the Moderates and **the civil** power **were on** the same side, so that forbearance, he felt, on the part **of the** Evangelicals, in the face of settlements forced at the point of the bayonet, need not now be urged.

"**I would like to do** injustice to no man," said M'Clymont magnanimously; "but **the** newspapers say something about **civil** rights. If ye can **clear** that up **to my mind,** Matha, ye **may** count me **on** your side."

"A plague on your civil rights! What have you **and me to do** wi' **civil** rights? We **want** peace, and ministers o' our ain choosing—is that no **enough?**"

"**But we maun** bide by the **law,** Matha. Patronage, **as I** understand it, is settled by the law o' the land, and **by it the** patron has certain rights— namely, the right **o'** giving a **place wi' a certain** income to a friend or **a** favourite. Now, I want to ken, **is** it just to interfere **wi'** ony man's rights that are established **by law?** Would ye like it yoursel', supposing ye **was** a patron?"

"But we're no patrons," cried the cartwright illogically, exhibiting signs of irritation. "If the law is onjust, are we to be overridden by an onjust law?"

"Then," said M'Clymont, rising, "I canna be a party to an unlawfu' thing. I'll be a Non-intrusionist, Matha, as sune as the wye is clear, for I dinna want my conscience meddled wi'; but until your law is altered in a fair and constitutional wye I'll bide as I am."

CHAPTER XXII.

PETER SHULE, THE BETHERAL.

It is a pleasing thing to see a man who has to discharge grave and responsible public functions condescending to unbend at times, and take a little lightsome recreation. The joint occupation of minister's man and sexton was not such as was calculated to foster levity of mind—the one necessitating a fairly uniform seriousness of character, and the other—going rather deeper—tending to depress the spirits. For long years Peter Shule, who performed these duties in the parish of Glenbuckie, had lived the lonely life of a single man. A singular change, however, had been observed in his manner of late: he had become less of a recluse, and he was sometimes overheard talking to himself in quite a jocose way. It is true, as he admitted, things had been a " heap busier i' the yaird," for, as he said, " that Non-intrusion fever had cuttet a guid wheen o' folk doon;" but to the thoughtful eye there was more elation in his manner than could be fairly derivable from consideration of a mere temporary briskness in business. Peter was a tall, thin, cadaverous man, with a face admirably adapted by nature for the vocation to which it had pleased Providence to call him. He was seldom observed to smile, and only once in the memory of the parish had he been known to laugh right out, and that was when he saw the mare "Brownie" yoked in Mrs. Lightbody's hearse approaching the kirkyard, with the great seven-feet coffin of the laird of Girtle, well secured with straw ropes, protruding half-way out of the box behind. The fact that Peter had been observed to laugh was remarked at the time, as much from the unprecedented nature of the occurrence, as from the untimeliness of the occasion. It may be that half a lifetime of grim humour was suddenly let loose by the novel, not to say unbecoming, character of the spectacle. But Peter's risible faculties had never been publicly exercised since, and it was felt that he might have to stow away many years' accumulation of light-heartedness before a suitable incident should again occur to set it free. Nevertheless, the betheral had a means of letting the immediate outer world know when he was in a tolerably happy frame of mind. This was indicated by a peculiar protuberance of the mouth, through which his breath was wont to come and go on these occasions in a kind of rhythmic measure, more or less distinct, according to the pressure of the pleasurable feeling by which, for the moment, he might be stirred.

His latest burial had been but a poor affair—namely, that of a pauper. His condition of mind, however, during the performance of his part of the last rites for this humble fellow-creature was unaccountably lightsome, so much so, that when it came to the tramping in of the earth at the conclusion of the ceremony, the muscles of his mouth gathered up joyously, and his breath, as the exercise increased, quickened to unmistakable palpitations of "Tullochgorum." However mercenary he might be in spirit, he was not so great an economist as to warrant the thought that such buoyancy was produced by the knowledge that this frail human burden to the parish had been safely secured under ground. The truth is he had recently been led to make occasional journeys over the knowe to the humble bothie of Widow M'Crone, the "'oo' leddy," as she was called. These visits were at first official, with the view of making the path straight for the minister, but latterly they had become voluntary and friendly. The betheral was naturally a shy creature, and seldom felt comfortable in female society; but Mrs. M'Crone was a woman of great adaptability of character, and had, in her intercourse with him, tapped a spring in his nature hitherto undiscovered. She was an ardent believer in omens, death-warnings, and the like, and was very knacky at laying out a corpse, or clearing up an ill dream. She had travelled much in Glenbuckie and neighbouring parishes. Her profession was that of a wool-gleaner. Leaving her home about the time of sheep-shearing, she would seek the sheep-tracks on the hillsides where the unshorn, heavily-coated sheep had left tufts of wool amongst the gorse and heather. This was the wool harvest which she gleaned day after day till her circuit was complete. In these journeys the 'oo' leddy was never ill-off for lodgings and comfortable fare. She was a kind of perambulating newspaper, always welcome at whatever farmer's ingle she chose to select for the night. On the completion of these annual journeys she would return home with a stock of wool which generally kept her spinning till the sheep-shearing season again returned. It was a fairly profitable and pleasant kind of life. As has been said, Peter's visits were at first official, but the widow was such a " prime cracker," that, by and by, he began to go over the knowe occasionally on his own account to spend the gloaming hour. Her personal reminiscences of " warnings" were thrilling to hear; a dog howling in the mirk, the dead bells tinkling in the ear, the glimpse of a passing wraith in the gloaming, a knock heard on the door of some sick person's room when no one was near, or the ticking of the death-watch in the middle of the night, all came within the range of her personal knowledge during her experience in lonely out-of-the-way farms. These warnings almost invariably foreshadowed death, or disaster of some kind more or less awful. Peter himself was not imaginative enough to have any superstitious fear. During the body-snatching period, when the parishioners had to take part in watching the graveyard, he was frequently hired as a substitute. To him this was not an unpleasant duty. Armed with a good box of snuff, a moderate supply of whisky, and the handle of an old spade, he would pass the contemplative night wandering over the familiar grassy mounds with a fair degree of mental evenliness.

Peter had a strong leaning towards the grim and ghastly side of things. He had never, however, got beyond material bounds. To him the power of being able to penetrate into the higher spiritual region seemed a great gift. The widow had more than once, by the exercise of her superior powers, told him beforehand of business that was coming his way, and it was not unnatural for a man who took an interest in his work to seek closer friendliness with one who could not only lead his mind to greater heights of awsomeness, but whose converse possessed such practical business advantages.

At the moment Peter was indulging in Tullochgorum, the 'oo' leddy had just returned from one of her tours. She had been away for about three weeks, and during this time he had pondered deeply over many things. He had dwelt particularly over the pleasant evenings he had spent at the bothie on the other side of the knowe, so when leaning on the wall, waiting for the pauper coffin, he heard from Jenny Sillishins, the henwife, that the 'oo' leddy had returned, he resolved to push through the interment as fast as decency would permit, and step over to the bothie that he might hear what fateful " ferlies" the oracle had to reveal.

The last clap having been given to the small earthen mound, Peter scraped the soil from his shoes with the spade, and took a near cut over the hill. His visit was not altogether unexpected, for the widow had charged the henwife to warn the betheral body that she was at home.

"So ye've won back," said Peter, when he had got fairly settled in the arm-chair which Mrs. M'Crone had placed for him beside the cheery fire.

"'Deed ay, Peter; it's true what the auld sang says: 'There's no place like home.'"

"And ye've gottin a braw pickle 'oo' this journey," continued Peter, ignoring sentiment.

"It was geyan plenty this turn," she replied, letting her eyes rest on the store of matted stuff which she had spread out on the floor to dry; "but it was a kind o' painfu' journey too, Peter. Ye'll no guess wha's won awa'?"

"No," said Peter, pursing up the muscles of his mouth, with some curiosity.

"Mrs. Whammond o' Mucklemains," replied the widow, with a sigh.

"They bury i' the next parish," said Peter, letting his chin fall and taking a consolatory pinch of snuff. "What would be the matter, na?"

"It was real sudden, Peter, real sudden; it cam owre her just like the clap o' a hand. But I kent fine something was gaun to happen."

"There noo, there would be some forecast, or something?"

"Ay, ye may weel say that. I was biding at the time wi' Mrs. Bengin o' the Ray, abune Mucklemains, when I heard the cock crawing twice i' the middle o' the night. I couldna sleep a wink, for I kent it was ill news, so I stole oot o' bed, and opened the back-door, and there I saw the creature standing on the top o' a wheel-less barrow, i' the thin munelight, just stretching his neck to craw for the third time, wi' his head turned in the direction o' Mucklemains."

"Keep and guide us! Did ye grip the beastie and feel his feet?"

"I did that, and eh, Peter, but they were cauld, a sure sign that there was news o' some trouble coming frae the gate his head pointed till. I gaed awa back to bed, and as I was lying doon the nock i' the kitchen chappet twelve o'clock. Weel, what do ye think? but just as I was telling Mrs. Bengin in the morning at breakfast, that I feared there would be ill news from Mucklemains, wha should come in but the ploughman, to tell us that the mistress had been ta'en awa' just at the turn o' the night."

"It's by-or'nar what's revealed to bruit beasts. That cock would ken fine, na," said Peter meditatively. "But did ye fin' muckle sickness i' the back-en' o' our ain parish, as ye cam through? This kirk-fever is putting a heap o' folk aff their or'nar."

"There is no muckle to complain o' yet," she said, "but as they can neither sleep nor eat for talking aboot this Speritual Independence, there's sure to be—— Mercy! did ye hear that?" Mrs. M'Crone drew her chair nearer to the betheral, and seized his arm. Peter at the moment believed she had seen a wraith or something, but as the spiritual dispensation must be meant for herself, he felt that any physical aid he could afford her would prove of little avail. He accordingly made no sign of offering protection.

"Did ye no hear it?" she inquired, after the first flutter of alarm was over—"something like somebody fisslin' ootside the door. Peter, ye maun come wi' me and see that there's nobody hiding aboot the place."

The "fisslin'" having been thus associated with possible flesh and blood, Peter was delighted to be looked up to as the champion of an unprotected woman. Seizing his bonnet, he walked boldly out into the grey gloaming, timidly followed by the agitated Mrs. M'Crone. They walked round the house, but no one was to be seen. Peter climbed on an inverted tub and looked into the water-barrel, to relieve her mind of the last possible fear.

"That is strange," she said.

"'Od, I hope it wasna a warning," remarked Peter, as they returned to the house and he reseated himself thoughtfully in the arm-chair. "For mysel' I dinna like thae warnings."

"Na, na, Peter; I ken the difference between a warning and a common fisslin' like yon. I could have laid my Bible-word there was somebody listening at the door. Do ye know, Peter, I have been getting real nervish of late."

"Ay," said the betheral, the corners of his mouth going down, "that's bad."

"Ever since I heard o' Leddy Sommeril's house being entered at the dead o' night. To think o' the body tied doon wi' ropes and the siller ta'en awa before her verra een!"

"Rich folk rin a deal o' risks," said Peter, failing to see the relevancy of her fears.

"Peter," she said, again laying her hand on his arm and speaking in confidential tones, "do you see that kist? Weel, there is as muckle siller in that kist as would mak' mony a man commit a great crime!"

"Lord bide wi' ye!" exclaimed the betheral, his pulse quickening. "Ye're no feart to tell us! Where did ye get it, 'oman?"

"Where did I get it? I got it by working for it —hard 'oo'-gathering and hard spinning. Would ye believe it, Peter: there are twenty gouden pound-pieces, and seven bonny white siller shillings, hidden awa' i' the shuttle o' that kist, and there's no another being i' the world kens o't but yoursel'?"

Peter was struck dumb by this unexpected and touching confidence. What a mint of money for this lone woman to possess, and no one to know of it but herself and him! Though Peter was very poor he had hitherto been an honest and virtuous man, but, it is true, his virtue and honesty had never been severely tried. This was perhaps the greatest temptation that had ever assailed him. For the moment his moral nature was in a state of chaotic bewilderment.

"Just think what might happen if ony dishonest body kent there was so much siller there!"

"True," remarked the betheral, "verra true." He felt honour and honesty were getting the upper hand in the moral confusion.

"Ye'll no wonder I feel easier i' my mind when ye step owre i' the darkening to spend an hour wi' me. Thieves are no near han' so ready looking near when they ken there is a man-body i' the house."

"No near han'," concurred Peter.

"Ye have sic a strong, deep voice," continued the widow, "that I sometimes think if ye were angry ye would maist fricht onybody."

The betheral sat up in his chair, and looked valorous, thinking the while of this poor woman's helplessness, and the soothing strength of his own protecting presence.

"Noo that the dark days are settling doon," proceeded the widow, "it's eerie wark biding a' by your lane wi' so muckle siller i' the hoose."

"It is that," admitted Peter. "I wouldna grudge to stand between you and danger if I could—but——"

"But what?" she inquired, as Peter paused, and seemed in a swither.

"Mrs. M'Crone," he said solemnly, and without the slightest show of sentiment, "we are twa lone bodies, you and me, and I think ye might be a heap safer if we bade thegither."

"Peter Shule!" she exclaimed, with virtuous emphasis, "what div ye mean?"

"Oh, I mean no offence," said Peter, willing to resile from the chivalrous position he had so suddenly assumed. "If it had been agreeable to you, I thought we might have got married—but never mind." Mrs. M'Crone looked up at him archly from the stool on which she sat, teasing her wool.

"Eh, Peter," she exclaimed, "who would ever have thought the like o' that? To think ye have been courting me a' this time and I didna ken o't, and then to lead me on so cunningly that I couldna hinder ye from making a proposal o' marriage."

"If ye think I can be of ony use to ye, I'm willing," said the betheral, keeping his mental eye steadily on the practical aspect of the question.

"Weel, Peter, it would be a great comfort to have ye aye i' the hoose wi' me, and now that ye have proposed I daurna say no to ye; but it was awfu' sly the wye ye did it. I suppose ye'll speak to the minister?"

"Weel," replied Peter, somewhat appalled at the rate at which events were hurrying on, "that will be the trying bit o't."

"Na, I'm sure he'll be weel pleased to ken ye're getting somebody who'll tak' real guid care o' ye. But," she said, rising to her feet, and placing one hand on his shoulder, patting his cheek the while with the other, "noo that I have lippened till ye, are ye quite sure it's mysel' ye want, and no the siller?"

The bridegroom-elect replied diplomatically, and on the following morning the parish received the startling news that there was a purpose of marriage between Peter Shule and Widow M'Crone.

CHAPTER XXIII.

THE DISRUPTION.

It was a memorable day that in 1843 when the guard of Her Majesty's mail-coach drew up in front of Nanse Tannock's change-house, and proclaimed to the assembled parishioners that the "ministers were oot." It was quite clear from the tone and look of the person making this proclamation that he was in full sympathy with the men who had taken this daring and decisive step. William Dickie, and one or two others, who not unfrequently got a "lift" to market on very reasonable terms from this good-natured functionary, expressed doubt as to whether it behoved a servant of Her Majesty to show such lightness of heart in speaking of an event which seemed to them like an act of rebellion against the established law of the country. The announcement, however, was cheered to the echo, and, as the coach drove away, the more thoughtful members of the crowd went inside to peruse the newspapers that had been left behind, and which contained full particulars of the important events that had just taken place in the Edinburgh ecclesiastical parliament. The more important facts were soon gleaned. The **Evangelical** ministers, **with the** venerable **Dr.** Chalmers **and Dr. Welsh at their** head, **had marched off from** the **presence of the Queen's** High Commissioner in **the** General **Assembly, leaving State** emoluments **for** ever behind **them. They had** inaugurated a **Free** Church Assembly, and 474 ministers had **solemnly** signed **a deed** demitting their charges. Then came **the** announcement, made by Dr. Chalmers, that **a** sum of £232,347 had been subscribed **towards the support** of ordinances in the **Free and spiritually independent** Church.

In the course of a **day or two a newspaper containing** a list **of** the **ministers who had left the** Establishment reached **the** parish, when **it was** known that Mr. Hyslop was amongst the seceders. **The same** night **a** meeting was held **in** Matha Spale's workshop. It was the largest gathering **ever** held in **the** village; and importance was attached **to** it from a knowledge of the fact that Robert **Simpson, and** one or two others who acted under his guidance, were to be present on the occasion. Up **to** this time Robert had held **aloof from the** Non-intrusion party, not from want of sympathy with them, but in the **hope that** Parliament would interfere between the conflicting courts—civil and ecclesiastical—and, by defining their different jurisdictions, put an end to the difficulties which had arisen. It was with great interest, therefore, that he awaited the result of Mr. Fox Maule's motion in the House of Commons, that an inquiry should be instituted into the grievances complained of. Robert considered Mr. Maule had taken the only fair and constitutional way out of the difficulty. His proposal was that the House should form itself into a Committee for the consideration of this great national question. He was aware that it was difficult at times to reconcile conflicting jurisdictions, but he could not admit that, when two courts equal by law, and by the Constitution independent of each other, came into conflict upon matters however trifling, or however important, one should assume to itself to say that the other was wrong. As he read the Constitution, it became Parliament to interfere. This proposal, which was opposed by Sir James Graham, the Solicitor-General, Sir Robert Peel, and other influential members of the House, was rejected by a large majority. To Robert Simpson the rejection of this motion seemed a great, as it was an unexpected calamity. He had hoped, if justice were to be had anywhere, it would be found in the calm and impartial Court of Parliament at Westminster; but as this hope had failed him, he felt he had no remedy left but the painful one of separating himself from the Church of his fathers.

There was great cheering as Robert Simpson and

Whinnyriggs walked into Matha Spale's workshop that evening, and took their places amongst the avowed adherents of the Free Church of Scotland. When silence had been restored, Matha Spale got to his feet, and said they would allow him the privilege in his own shop of proposing that Robert Simpson should take the chair. From Robert's presence at the meeting he was sure he had settled in his mind to take their side. They were all, he was sure, proud to see him, and he was equally sure they could not be under the guidance of a better chairman. Robert was carried into this position by the unanimous voice of the meeting. Having given out four verses of a Psalm, which was led by the powerful voice of Whinnyriggs, and further, having constituted the meeting in a most becoming and solemn manner, the chairman stood up to address the assembly.

While Robert Simpson proceeded with his address, Major Macilorum was marching down the kirk brae, accompanied by Will Loadstone the carrier, and Tammas Scougall the mole-catcher. The Major, who heard of the proposed gathering late in the day, determined to be present with such a following as he could muster, to protest, in the Queen's name, against what he believed to be a violation of common-sense, if not an act of open rebellion against constituted authority. The Major, who was flushed with the walk, and with the excitement of the enterprise, marched into the cartwright's yard and announced his presence by three sharp knocks on the door of the workshop with the handle of his stick. There was great consternation amongst a section of the audience as the florid countenance of the warlike Major was observed at the open door. The dim forms of the carrier and the mole-catcher, as they stood behind him in the grey of the gloaming, were believed by some to be the advance-guard of a regiment of soldiers, who would be satisfied with nothing less than unconditional capitulation.

"Go on with your deliberations if they are lawful," cried the Major, as the chairman paused and the audience stared.

"We need no command to do that," replied the cartwright, stepping towards and facing the intruder; "but first of a' tell me what purpose ye are here for. Is it peace or war?"

"I am essentially a man of war in a physical sense," answered the Major. "I have always been at war also with ignorance, cant, hypocritical sanctimoniousness, senseless secession, and with every form of fanatical immoderation; but I am not here to draw the civil sword. The time is past for settling matters of belief in that way. But I am here in name of Her Majesty the Queen, for the purpose of lodging my solemn protest against this shameful overthrow of the Established Kirk. Have you a chairman?"

"I am chairman," said Robert Simpson, stretching his tall form to its full height, nothing daunted. "But perhaps the gallant Major will sit down peacefully, and listen to what we have to say before he protests against it."

"I know the purpose of the meeting, and that is enough for me. I am not here to bandy words with you, but if such disloyal acts are to go down to posterity, they must be accompanied by the fact that I, Major Macilorum, raised my solemn protest against them." Whereupon this fiery son of Mars marched up the workshop floor, placed his written protest in the hands of the chairman, at the same time calling upon his two followers to witness that he had done so. This accomplished, he bowed ceremoniously to the representative head of the meeting, and walked out of the door. While the chairman read over the protest to himself, the meeting relieved its pent-up feelings in oral speculation as to what the action of the Major might lead to.

"A protest in name o' the Queen," said Haplands. "'Od, it really looks like a serious affair!"

"A serious affair," echoed M'Alpine, who sat within hearing.

"He talked aboot a ceevil sword," remarked Tullochmains. "What, na, do ye think that might mean? I never could see much ceevility about swords or guns, for my pairt."

"Ay man, Tulloch, I noticed that too," cried

M'Alpine. "Dagont! if there is to be ony pains or penalties aboot this Disruption business I think we should let it abee."

The conversation was interrupted by the chairman clearing his throat.

"The Major is a decent fellow," he began, "and while his protest may clear his own conscience, it can have no effect in altering our purpose, for it is simply a repetition in his own vigorous terms of the old Moderate arguments that we know so well."

"But," ventured Haplands, "it was in name o' the Queen, was it no? We can gang a certain length, ye ken, but we canna afford to gang against the Queen, and lose our places." Mrs. Haplands, who sat beside her husband, was not quite clear on this point herself, and was rather proud to hear her husband raise his voice amongst so many people in this manly way.

The chairman having explained the meaning of the Major's protest, and having given assurance of its utter harmlessness as a legal instrument, proceeded with his remarks.

It was needful, he said, to set things straight, so far as he was concerned, by explaining how he came to be there. He hadn't liked the look of things, especially since the Court of Session had taken on themselves to say what was spiritual independence and what was not. He couldn't believe that the Lords of Session were the proper judges of matters spiritual; still, he had hoped that justice would **be** done, and that the voice of the Church would in the end be permitted to rule in her own affairs, but this had been denied her. **From the** decision recently come **to** there was no appeal, and he, for one, would never submit **to** remain in a Church where the right of private judgment in matters of such great importance to the people was entirely set aside by the secular power. (Great applause.)

"We may have been prepared, for **the sake** of peace, to make concessions," continued the chairman, warming under these tokens of approbation, "**but** there is a limit, and, in my opinion, that limit **has** been seriously overstepped; and we **can no longer** remain as we are, and respect ourselves **as a free and** independent people. For myself, I **tell you, it** has been a bitter struggle, this breaking of the **old ties.** The associations o' the past have been very sacred to **me, as** I have no doubt they are to you all. It has taken a stiff wrench, I can tell ye; **but** now that the thing has been done, we must be true to our principles, we must stick together and be **true** to each other, and show to the world, at whatever sacrifice to ourselves, that we are in earnest; and that the course we have taken is not a mere threat, which we are afraid or unwilling to carry out."

When the chairman sat down there was a general call for Matha Spale. The cartwright rose in his place, with great deliberation. Any one could see by his face and manner it was a stern sense of duty, and no mere desire for personal glorification, that induced him to get to his feet.

"Ye a' ken I'm nae speaker," he said slowly, but with a determination of tone which showed he would not shirk his fair share of the work they had met to get through. "I would work twal' hours in a saw-pit ony day rather than stand up and mak' a speech, which is a thing I have no gift for doing. Still-an-on, we are a' here earnest and serious-minded folk, and somebody maun do the speaking. Noo, first and foremost, I'll just tell ye what is bunemost on my mind, and let ye judge for yoursel's. I was busy the day wi' the adze on the shaft o' Drakemyre's new cart, and had my head doon owre the wark, when somebody entered the shop. I thought it was Eneas M'Clymont, and wasna in a hurry looking up, but it turned out to be the factor, Mr. Cunningham. I lifted my bonnet, and speired for his family in a friendly wye. 'Oh, they're weel enough,' he said, geyan dry-like. After a while he said, 'Matha, I hear ye are taking a forward part wi' these Evangelicals.' 'Weel,' says I, 'suppose I am; wha's business is that?' 'You are his Lordship's tenant,' says he; 'and his Lordship is on the ither side.' 'Weel,' says I, 'let his Lordship bide on the ither side; wha's trying to bring him owre? I have only a lease o' the property. His Lordship is quite free to believe what he likes for me.'

"'But leases will come to an end,' he said. 'Besides, his Lordship is a guid customer.'

"'D—n a' such customers,' says I, for I was angert. 'Didn't he put the place into the market when my last lease was out, and didn't I get it because I was the highest bidder? As for your wark, I gie ye guid value for your money, and if ye think ye can get a cheaper and a better job ony ither place, ye are free to gang.'"

"Bright, Matha!" cried Whinnyriggs, his face gleaming with approval. "That was weel pitched into him."

"Barring the sweerin'," said Haplands correctively.

"I admit it was a hasty answer," continued Matha, "but I was in a bleezin' rage at the time, and forgot mysel' a'thegither, so he just turns on his heel. 'I was inclined to speak friendly to ye,' says he, 'and gie ye guid advice, but since ye'll no listen to reason, ye may put your hoose in order; ye needna think to despise the authority o' your superiors. It is true, ye have a tack that confers the right o' using the place as a workshop, but ye have turned it into a rendezvous o' sedition; and as ye have despised friendly warning, we must e'en see what the law will say on the subject.' 'Aweel,' says I, 'we'll tak' oor risk.'"

"Bravely spoken!" cried Whinnyriggs. "The fussy body is aye meddling wi' somebody."

"Now," said Matha, "I 'm a heap easier sin' I have gotten this thing off my mind. For my pairt, I 'm nane feart. The shop answers me weel enough, but I am giein' a decent rent for it, and if I have to shift there 's nobody but the mistress and me to suffer; still, it shows to what lengths things may be driven in this great creesis. I 'll no say but he may be tryin't on wi' ithers, besides mysel', but gin we a' stan' thegither like ae mân, as the chairman has advised, and show that we are ready, if need be, to mak' sacrifices for what we think right, we are sure to get the upper hand i' the long-run."

From the enthusiasm with which the cartwright's remarks were received there seemed little danger of the cause failing from lack of unanimity. Haplands and his friends, ashamed of their recent weakness, shuffled loudly with their feet to show to what extent their bravery could go.

"I have little fear but the noble Lord, whose tenants most of us are, can respect consistency," continued Matha. "We may differ frae him in politics, and in matters religious, but he 'll no be true to the principles o' the House o' Killie if he stoops to do an onjust thing. Noo we maun come to business. Some o' ye would maybe see frae the newspapers that an uncommon thing had happened while the Queen's High Commissioner was receiving the members o' Assembly at Holyrood Palace. Before proceeding to open the reverend court, the picture o' King William was seen to move on the wa', then it fell wi' an awsome crash. It was an uncanny omen. What could that mean, think ye? It was a gey odd thing that the picture o' the king who had restored the Presbyterian religion and Speritual Independence to Scotland should come doon at that creetical moment. I'm no ane that would be carried awa' wi' superstitious freits, yet I canna but alloo that there was something i' the fa'in' of the effigy o' King William, to gie us heartenin' that we're on the true side. For mysel', I look on it as a sign, and I think it would have been a guid thing for the Moderates if they had ta'en the same view; but the thing is dune, the picture has fa'en; we have flung off the bonds o' Erastian rule, and we are now free." Matha was getting heated to the work, and so was his audience, for while he paused to wipe away the perspiration from his face he was greeted with enthusiastic cheering. "Weel," he continued, "what are we now to do? We maun choose a minister. Thank God, we are free to do that. No court o' law i' the country can hinder us in oor choice noo. There is one man who has taken a fearless place in this Disruption-battle—ye a' ken his name,—for he has come here in the verra teeth o' the powers that be, and against their will, to give us instruction and mak' the wye plain to us. We see from the newspapers that he has been true to his colours. He has thrown aff the graith and coupet the cart o' worldly comforts at the door o' the State, regairdless o' what may happen to himsel'. Noo, folk, would it no be pleasing to ye to have such a man to be your minister? Mr. Hyslop kens a' the oots and ins o' the principles we have focht for, and as we are here to select some ane to be our speritual guide, for my pairt I think we couldna secure a better man."

"Maister Chairman," said Haplands from his corner, in a subdued voice; "wouldna we need a kirk, a schule-room, or something to put a minister in?"

"True," answered Matha, feeling that he had not yet brought matters to a thoroughly practical issue. "What Haplands says is right, but let us get the minister first, and I'll be bound we'll no be lang in getting a meeting-hoose. Mr. Hyslop is no the man to let the grass grow under his feet. Meantime, in spite o' the threats I have heard this day, my workshop is open to ye. The Author o' oor religion was brought up Himsel' in a carpenter's shop, and I canna but think it would be an appropriate thing that the first Free Kirk congregation in Glenbuckie should, for a time at least, meet in a similar place. Noo, maybe I've said a' I should say, by way o' clearin' the grund; but before I sit doon I have to propose that the Rev. Mr. Hyslop be invited to become the first Free Kirk minister o' Glenbuckie."

Whinnyriggs jumped to his feet as the cartwright sat down, and in a word seconded this proposal, which was carried by acclamation.

Meantime Major Macilorum, troubled in mind as to the effect his protest might have on the meeting, sent his witnesses home, and went along to Nanse Tannock's to see the *Times*, which had that day arrived—a fortnight old. The Major's study of the newspaper was made the means of passing the time till the meeting should terminate. On his way home he overtook M'Alpine, who was quietly pacing up the brae towards his own loaning. The Major sounded a halt by coughing in rather a peremptory way.

"Well," he cried sternly, when he came to where the farmer stood at the angle leading off the main road to his own farm, "what did you people think of my protest?"

"Dod, it was a real courageous thing," said M'Alpine, in a pacific mood. "Ye frichtit some o' them, I can tell ye." He was afraid to tell this impulsive man of war that it had not been read to the meeting.

"You backed it up, I hope?"

"Weel, ye see, what would the voice o' wan man be against such an uncommon multitude as yon?"

"One man, sir? Why, one man has altered the opinions and the condition of half a continent before now. I suppose they would adjourn to consider it?"

"That would 'a been a sensible thing; but, Major, ye see, Matha Spale and a wheen mair were so set on this Maister Heeslop frae Beith, that, richt reason or nane, they bit to gie him a call in spite o' a' that might be said."

"And they have seceded from the established religion of the country?" cried the Major, rapping his stick threateningly on the macadamised road. (Macadam was a native of the county, and had lately exercised his art on this special road.)

"Ay, I'm sorry to say 't."

For some seconds after this the air around the farmer's head snapped and crackled with sharp wrathful snorts, mingled with language of the most profane and abusive character; so much so that poor M'Alpine, who aimed at being all things to all men, felt within himself that he was but ill fitted to bear an independent share in this ungenerous and controversial world. As he went up the loaning the stars came out, and smiled peacefully in the blue canopy overhead. There, he thought within himself, it would be pleasant to dwell, for in that peaceful region there is neither Whig nor Tory, Moderate nor Evangelical.

CHAPTER XXIV.

THE MINISTER'S RECORD (*concluded*).

ALAS! alas! who would have thought that the words of a poor demented spae-woman should have been charged with such deep prophetic significance? Profound trouble, of a truth, has come upon us; but I thank the Lord that it has come as she foretold, from without. In my more immediate family circle there is much to sustain and cheer me; and, to speak with strict accuracy, there is need for such sustenance and cheer, for from without there is sore and grievous trouble pressing upon us. The Church, alas! is rent asunder. The Evangelicals have, indeed, taken their departure in much greater numbers than was expected, and last Sabbath I preached a sermon to a congregation consisting of my wife, the twin bairns, my lawful serving-woman, William Dickie, and Peter Shule, the betheral. William Dickie came round to the vestry when I was taking off my gown, and told me he fully expected M'Clymont, the blanket-weaver, and M'Alpine, to be present; but it seems, after all, they followed the multitude and went down to hear the gospel according to the Free Church, as preached in Matthew Spale's workshop. It is painful to think how the people have slipped away clean out of my hands, how they have deserted their ancient faith, and with it relinquished all respect for those who minister in the sacred courts where they were wont to worship. This was painfully brought to my mind the other day, as I passed through the village to visit a poor body who had received the sad news that her son had been drowned on his first voyage to the Indies. Some half dozen laddie-weans were sitting by the roadside, scraping together all the rubbish and road glaur they could find within reach. They seemed so eident over their task that I could not help pausing to see what they were about—feeling, now that I have a family of my own, some interest in bairnies' ploys.

"Well, laddies," I said quite affably, as I placed my hand on the fair curly pow of the biggest boy, "what are you about?"

"We are bigging a kirk," said the callant, real earnest-like.

"Building a kirk, are you, my laddie? Well, that is a fine thing to do; let me see."

He turned to the work with some pride. "There is the wa's, and the galleries; and this is the pu'pit, ye see."

I could not help admiring the contrivance and

skill of the callant, who spoke with such ready enthusiasm about the good work in which he was engaged.

"But," I said encouragingly, "where is the minister? If you have a kirk, you must have a minister."

"Weel, sir, ye see we hadna as muckle dirt left as would mak' a minister."

Poor, simple, innocent bairnies! I don't think their bonny clear-eyed spokesman meant the least disrespect by this irreverent remark, but, all the same, I proceeded on my way with a sad heart, and I could not help pondering, as I went down the village street, on the great change that had come over the spirit of my once docile and contented people, for it seemed to me almost as if these guileless laddie-weans, sitting at their play by the syver-edge, were only repeating to my face such words of bitterness and disrespect as they might have learned from the lips of grown-up partisans at home.

For several weeks after the once solid ranks of the Established Kirk had been broken by the secession of the Evangelicals, my wife and I were afflicted with great heaviness of heart, not knowing what might betide. It is true, the emoluments might remain, though even that was doubtful, for there was much talk about re-arrangement of charges, and so forth; but even if the emoluments did remain, it was a bitter thing to think I was almost wholly deprived of my flock. Major Macilorum had written me a kind and hearty letter, stating that as the minister of the other parish had deserted his colours, he, the Major, had now decided to remain no longer on neutral ground, but would come over and worship with me. This was certainly kind, but it was at best a poor, not to say an unreliable, accession to a congregation that numbered less than a dozen souls. It has, however, been averred with truth, that the darkest hour is that which precedes the dawn. The Great Disposer of events was working silently during this period of darkness. He had doubtless heard our spiritual groaning, for, just when we were in our sorest plight of apprehension and mental perturbation, Her Majesty's post-runner, Sandy Colquhoun, came to my door one morning, while I was in my study extending some notes which I thought would dovetail suitably into my projected book on "Popular Social Sins." I answered the lad's knock myself, for of late we had been doing without a nursemaid, and as my pulpit preparation was now less severe, I felt it a duty to put my hand to, and do any odd turn that would leave my wife and the serving-woman freer for the extra household duties now devolving upon them. The lad put a large official-looking letter, bearing the London postmark, into my hand. I could see at a glance that it was from my noble friend and patron, the Earl of Killie; for in truth his name was inscribed in clear bold letters on the corner of the envelope. It was as kind a letter as ever was penned. The factor, it appears, had informed his Lordship of the disloyalty to Established Church principles in the parish, and of the shameful secession which had taken place under my ministry. That he had not forgotten my " good offices in connection with the great cause which he and all good Moderate men had at heart, the enclosed would testify." The document he enclosed was a presentation in my favour to the parish of Kilmallie. When I got this length I could see no more, for the tears came to my eyes at the thought of how the Lord had opened up a way out of the darkness for myself and young helpless family. When my wife came into my study to learn the news—for she had seen the post lad going down the avenue—I handed the missives to her, for I was so overcome that speech failed me. When she had encompassed their meaning she threw herself on my neck, and for a space we clung to each other and wept aloud together for joy.

The matter is all settled now. I have been to Kilmallie, and truly I received a most kind and cordial welcome. The congregation has stood true to their religion as established by law, and though their minister saw it to be his duty to go over to the other side, only a handful, so to speak, of the people, went with him, leaving the session intact, and I am bound to say they seem to me a set of sober-minded, intelligent, God-fearing men.

Kilmallie is pleasantly situated in a fine agricultural district overlooking the sea. There is a fine manse, and glebe-lands, ample, I am told, to feed a score of sheep and graze a couple of cows. Truly "the lines have fallen to me in pleasant places," as the Psalmist says. My old sermons will stand me in good stead for many a day to come; and as I shall consequently have much time for study, who knows but from this quiet rural spot may issue a work on popular social transgressions, that may not only draw many eyes to the place, but, what is of infinitely more value, help to turn the tide of error backward, and lead many to seek that wisdom whose ways are ways of pleasantness, and whose paths are paths of peace.

In a simple and truthful chronicle of events which have occurred in my own parish and my own time, such as this purports to be, it would ill beseem me to omit, on party grounds, an incident that has given cause for great joy and rejoicing to the Free Church congregation at present holding their diets of worship in the cartwright's workshop. It seems that two or three days after the disruption of the Kirk, the mistress of Girtle was suddenly smitten down with a serious malady. Poor Girzie, like her late brother, had always more regard for the things that are seen and temporal than for things that are unseen and eternal; so when her illness took an alarming turn, she packed off Sandy Speirs to fetch her, not a minister of the gospel, as might have been expected, but a lawyer body from Ayr. This, as I understood, was to make her will; and, indeed, the thing was not done a day too soon, for in less than a week's time the poor woman had passed hence, and was no more. When the will was read subsequently, it was found that after setting aside a portion for Sandy Speirs and Betty M'Clymont, and a small marriage dowry for Robert Simpson's only daughter, the whole residue of her estate, without restriction, was left for behoof of the Glenbuckie Free Church congregation, "to be applied by the session and deacons' court of said church for the time being, as they shall see proper to determine." To a poor moneyless Church like that which had just been constituted this remarkable benefaction must have been most welcome and opportune. This bequest, I believe, was due to the influence of Robert Simpson, who, it is said, generously advised that it should be made over to the Church party with whom he had cast in his lot. From a knowledge of the testatrix I can well believe this is not outwith the truth, for truly she was a woman of great nearness in her giving to the cause of religion. It certainly could not be said of her that she "loved the gates of Zion more than the dwellings of Jacob"! Indeed, I am convinced in my own mind that she never would have left her money to the Church at all had it not been put into her head. Robert Simpson is a man I shall never fail to respect, for though we have differed at times in our views as to doctrinal points, Church-government, and the like, he has never ceased to be friendly. When my household was down with the smittle trouble, to which I have already alluded in these pages, he was the only man in the parish who sent regularly to my door to inquire for the poor suffering bairns. He has, it is true, gone over to the other side, but he is not a man to allow minor ecclesiastical differences of opinion to break up private friendships. When he had finally made up his mind to leave the Established Kirk, he came to the manse and explained that his quarrel was with the State and not with me. He considered our differences of opinion were not such as should interfere with the regard we bore for each other; and when my wife, who was present during the conversation, had set down the toddy things (she has now greatly changed in respect to these matters), he took up his glass and paid a most feeling tribute to my wife and myself, and hoped so earnestly, and I might say eloquently, that the hinges of friendship would never rust, that the tears welled into my eyes, and almost unfitted me for making a suitable reply.

I have just received a letter intimating that the

Presbytery have fixed the day for my **induction.** The dinner is to take place in **the Cross Keys Inn,** Kilmallie, immediately after the service. For **my** part, I have but small relish for induction or ordination dinners. **I am not** quite sure that they are a fitting **termination to such a** solemn service; for truly **it** is painful to see reverend fathers and brethren—eminent Moderate divines—casting aside their moderation as soon as the toddy-bowl is set upon **the** table. I have often found in my heart **to raise my** solemn testimony against these social excesses, **but** I suppose it would be considered ill-judged taste to do so at my own induction.

This near prospect **of** separation from old friends and old associations, while **most desirable for me in** my present circumstances, **has impressed my mind** with grave and solemn reflections. Verily **we are** but silly creatures at the best, easily up and as easily down. Popularity is as **a wave of** the **sea;** to-day **we are borne** high in triumph on its majestic bosom, to-morrow it has receded, and we are stranded, helpless **on** an unfriendly and barren shore. We **are but** strangers and pilgrims upon the earth. Here we have no continuing city, and it **is well** when we can apply such lessons, and lay hold of a habitation which hath foundations, whose builder **and** maker is God. These wholesome, moral, and spiritual contemplations have helped me to set aside all feelings of animosity. The other day I met the

Rev. Mr. Hyslop on the roadway, just outside of Mrs. Tannock's door. I was overwhelmed for the moment with embarrassment and indecision, but it was soon over; my better nature soon gained the mastery, and I went straight up to him, gave him the right hand of fellowship, and bade him kindly welcome to the parish. I am truly glad that I did so, for I found him a most friendly, good-hearted, Christian man. After all, who can tell but the Lord Himself has been overturning the Church for wise and gracious purposes?

William Dickie, who, since my presentation to Kilmallie, has some thought of going over to the other side, informs me that many who never darkened the door of a place of worship before are now found flocking to the cartwright's workshop on the Lord's Day; prominent amongst these is that little radical tailor body who formerly gave no small concern and trouble to my predecessor, Rev. Dr. Plunket. On the whole, this is not surprising to me, for my wife, who was a regular visitor of the family, informed me that a great change had come over him for the better since the death of that poor, erring creature, Maggie Winlestrae. In spite of this change in the character of the man, I believe he had too much radical blood in his veins ever to seek admission to any Church connected with the State. It is therefore a providential thing that any Church has been set up to take such characters in.

There remains now but little more to say in bringing this record to a close. There have been great upturnings in the manse for many days. The betheral, and the 'oo' leddy, now man and wife, have been of great service to us in packing and tying things together. My wife thoughtfully procured half a dozen potato-barrels for the preservation and protection of my books, the packing of which in the first instance fell to my own hand. Manual labour, however, is a thing I am but ill fitted for. I worked so eidently at the task that my back ached till I thought it would break, but when my wife came in and found I had the barrels stuffed full and the half of the books still to pack, she called Peter Shule into the room, and good-naturedly ordered him to undo all I had done, and with her own hand, by dint of skilful arrangement, managed with wondrous neatness to stow away every book I possessed. By her advice I did not interfere with the work any more. Now that the separation is near at hand, the hearts of the people seem to be softening towards me. Though the harvest is yellow in the fields and ripe for the sickle, Whinnyriggs and M'Alpine have both offered to send me a couple of carts each, with strong, willing serving-men to convey my goods and chattels to Kilmallie, which is a great journey, and cannot consume less than two days' and two nights' time in going and returning. Mrs. Tannock also proffered me the use of her chaise to convey my family to their future home free of charge, but as Lord Killie had instructed the factor to put his Lordship's own carriage at our disposal for that purpose, Mrs. Tannock's considerate service was not required.

William Dickie tried to put it into my head that such kindness on behalf of my late parishioners was open to suspicion, inasmuch as it effected my removal from the parish, but I do not think this surmise is consistent with the truth; indeed, I believe it is a very unkind and ungenerous suspicion; and my wife, who has wondrous insight into character, avers that it is neither more nor less than a mean method of trying to cover his own niggardly conduct in not having offered to lend us a helping hand. It is not for me, however, to judge any man's motives.

I have only one incident more to relate and then I am done. The schoolmaster lad did a real kindly and thoughtful thing. My wife, who has great relish for, and sympathy with, poetic literature, has long thought highly of the lad's gifts. It seems he had been exercising his pen with regard to recent events in the parish in a little ballad entitled "The Scattering of the Sheep." One day my wife brought the youth into my study that I might hear a recitation of the lines from his own lips, and when I saw him standing up before me, eloquently reading pathetic verses of his own making that referred to myself and my poor dispersed flock, I was greatly overcome.

My wife tells me **he means** to send the ballad to *Tait's Edinburgh Magazine,* **and if it** should appear, **which** I think is most likely, **I shall** cut **it out** and preserve it in a frame, as a touching memorial of my well-intended but unsuccessful **labours in** the parish **of** Glenbuckie.

THE END.

Printed by T. and A. CONSTABLE, Printers to Her Majesty, *at the Edinburgh University Press.*

www.ingramcontent.com/pod-product-compliance
Lightning Source LLC
Chambersburg PA
CBHW032045230426
43672CB00009B/1482